TIME-SAVING TRAINING
for Multisport Athletes

Rick Niles, MA

Rick Niles Multi-Sport Fitness, Santa Rosa, CA

Human Kinetics

Library of Congress Cataloging-in-Publication Data

Niles, Rick, 1946-
     Time-saving training for multisport athletes /
     Rick Niles.
          p.   cm.
     Includes index.
     ISBN 0-88011-538-6
     1. Triathlon--Training.   2. Track and field athletes--Training of.
     I. Title.
     GV1060.73.N55   1997
     796.42--dc20
                                                             96-31260
                                                             CIP

ISBN: 0-88011-538-6

Acquisitions Editor: Kenneth Mange; **Developmental Editor:** Kristine Enderle; **Assistant Editors:** Sandra Merz Bott, Coree Schutter; **Copyeditor:** Bob Replinger; **Proofreader:** Debra Aglaia; **Indexer:** Barbara E. Cohen; **Graphic Designer:** Robert Reuther; **Graphic Artist:** Sandra Meier; **Photo Editor:** Boyd LaFoon; **Cover Designer:** Jack Davis; **Photographer (cover):** © Unicorn Stock Photography/Aneal Vohra; **Illustrators:** Paul To, line art; Jennifer Delmotte, Mac art; **Printer:** United Graphics

Human Kinetics books are available at special discounts for bulk purchase. Special editions or book excerpts can also be created to specification. For details, contact the Special Sales Manager at Human Kinetics.

Printed in the United States of America

10   9   8   7   6   5   4   3   2   1

Human Kinetics
Web site: http://www.humankinetics.com/

United States: Human Kinetics, P.O. Box 5076, Champaign, IL 61825-5076
1-800-747-4457
e-mail: humank@hkusa.com

Canada: Human Kinetics, Box 24040, Windsor, ON N8Y 4Y9
1-800-465-7301 (in Canada only)
e-mail: humank@hkcanada.com

Europe: Human Kinetics, P.O. Box IW14, Leeds LS16 6TR, United Kingdom
(44) 1132 781708
e-mail: humank@hkeurope.com

Australia: Human Kinetics, 57A Price Avenue, Lower Mitcham, South Australia 5062
(08) 277 1555
e-mail: humank@hkaustralia.com

New Zealand: Human Kinetics, P.O. Box 105-231, Auckland 1
(09) 523 3462
e-mail: humank@hknewz.com

Contents

Foreword

Time-Saving Training for Multisport Athletes is the book that I wanted to write. As I perused the advance copy, I found myself thinking repeatedly, "This is so true!" Rick Niles's philosophy of a good training program shares many of the ideas I have, as I read in his highlighted ideas and summaries. I have never been one to pile on the miles just for the sake of bragging rights when triathletes compare their training logs. On the contrary, I am a proud minimalist (make that "minimilist") when it comes to training. I train as a means to an objective, and that objective is to race faster the next time than I did the last time—faster, hopefully, than all my competitors, too! This improvement can come only through a structured, well-planned, training regimen. As Rick emphasizes in this book, "It is not a matter of *how much* you train, but of *how* you train."

I entered my first triathlon in 1984 on a borrowed bike, a wing, and a prayer. I was fortunate to be coming off four years of college swimming and three years of spring track, but my bike training had consisted solely of riding the few miles to and from work (that is, until my bike was stolen the day before the race!). That first race, however, kicked off a 13-year professional career that still is on the upswing: In 1995 I had my best season ever by winning both the ITU World Championships at the Olympic distance and the Hawaiian Ironman World Championships.

These titles would not have been possible had I not made a full-time commitment, but I didn't start out as a full-time professional. During my first five years' racing in the pro division, I also worked full-time for a consulting firm and learned firsthand the need for time-saving training. I was able to compete head-to-head with full-time athletes through training smarter—instead of longer—since I simply didn't have time to spare. I learned to make good use of my lunch hour and to choose quality over quantity for workouts. For five years I continued to improve, though my training time averaged only 12 hours a week.

When my company went bankrupt in 1989, I had the choice of looking for a new job or going for it full-time on the professional circuit. I am happy to report that my work résumé is still collecting dust. My training time has now increased to some 20 to 25 hours weekly, but many of the principles that I learned when I was trying to get the most out of the least time still hold true. Because my rest time now has increased substantially, I can train longer and still recover. It would have been a huge mistake to attempt my current training volume while I was still working: I would certainly have broken down physically—and probably mentally as well.

A triathlete who will endure must learn to balance work, family, and other parts of daily life with a manageable training and racing schedule. Many people think this compromise in training time will bring lackluster results and a slide in performance. But it is possible to continue to improve on as little as five to nine hours a week of training. In addition, the reduction in stress from leading a more balanced lifestyle may bring even greater gains. It is the structure of these training hours that is critical.

When I first began training for triathlon, there were few coaches experienced in multisport training and virtually no books on the subject. I learned what I could by trial and error and drawing on my previous single-sport background. If I could have read this book in my early days, it certainly would have brought me to a higher level in half the time. So much is now known about threshold training, training in cycles, recovery, carbohydrate-replacement, overtraining, and tapering that I could only learn the hard way. *Time-Saving Training for Multisport Athletes* covers it all in a straightforward, understandable format.

Few people have the talent, means, or desire to compete and race full-time. For the vast majority, triathlon is a hobby, but a hobby that many take very seriously. If you are willing to commit five to nine hours a week to triathlon, you owe it to yourself to get the most out of your training that you can. With a balanced, structured program, like the ones outlined here, you can become a faster and fitter triathlete and still have time and energy to devote to the rest of your life—ensuring that you will also be a happier triathlete.

Karen Smyers

Preface

Have you ever stood at the starting line of some event thinking, "This time, something magical is going to happen"? You expect old barriers and finish times to fall like hail stones in Kansas. You don't know why—you just know it will happen—or hope it will. But soon into the endeavor, you begin to realize that those old barriers and finish times are quite alive and well. It might be a good or bad day, but it won't be particularly remarkable. Sure, you have magical moments. But you had better pay attention: They come and go quickly. More often you are stuck at a constant level of performance. You consistently put in your time or miles, but little changes. "Well," you think, "if I had more time. . . ." But there is no more time. No matter how much you want it, you just can't rub the lamp and have a 36-hour day.

You can, however, change your performance level. You don't need genies or lamps, and you don't need to quit your job—you only need five to nine hours a week. Changes in your fitness level come most readily from training to your own level of abilities. This is a book explaining how to become the best athlete that you can be. You have personal time constraints, strengths, and weaknesses. You want to use your time and ability as efficiently as possible. *Time-Saving Training for Multisport Athletes* will show you how to train for swimming, cycling, and running, fitting it all in with the rest of your life. The system you'll find outlined here is designed to help average people become a little less so.

This is a book for people who enjoy competing in multisport events for fun. Pleasure can simply be finishing an event. It can be beating an old finishing time or winning in your age group. You define what is fun.

Fitness improvements sometimes come very quickly, sometimes not so fast. Patterns and degrees of change in fitness are as individual as fingerprints. If you follow the system in this book, you will get faster. You will probably never be as fast as some people, but you will always be faster than others. One simple fact will endure: When you improve at anything, you enjoy it more.

Even more coaches now prescribe workouts by time rather than distance. We will look at how to best split up your time. In training for three sports, most people will see performance improvements by training nine hours or less weekly. It's amazing what you can do with five hours. People training for Ironman events will need to spend more hours some weeks, but they still will see fitness improvements from nine-hour weeks. You can cut your Ironman training in half, keeping it in the nine-hour range, and as low as five hours weekly, and still finish an international or sprint-distance triathlon with dignity. Training routines of more than nine hours might look good on paper, but they often are left uncompleted. Most of us can spare an hour or two a day, but not much more. In *Time-Saving Training for Multisport Athletes*, we approach training from the standpoint that it doesn't take *more* training to achieve the end, but rather certain kinds of training done at particular times. It is quality training, or better, *specific* training.

To improve fitness in a limited time, workouts must have a purpose. Some workouts are meant to be slow, others fast. Some are hard and others are easy. A slow workout may not be easy, and a fast workout may not seem hard. *The intensity of training must vary according to the intent for each session.* The sample training weeks will show you how to put together a schedule. The underlying principles are constant, whether you want to achieve better fitness for its own sake, compete in two events a year, or become a regular warrior.

I came to write this book because almost all the people who have consulted me for training have come with the same problem: No fitness changes are occuring. They don't get faster, and it doesn't get any easier. Although they assume more training must be better, that often isn't the solution—to fitness or most other things. Initially, it is difficult to convince people they need to train *less*. At first, they worry, and a few people don't know what to do with the extra time! Sure. As they begin to see performance changes, the time gets shuffled somewhere else. Like extra money, surplus time rapidly disappears.

Arbitrary goals can lead to frustration. A simple analytical system, however, can show if you will make any real gains from a workout. By seeing a pattern of progression, you will be able to hone your goals realistically. Throughout this book you will find interesting time-saving tips to help you squeeze in some of those workouts that are often pushed from your day's schedule. You will understand what it takes to make fitness changes. You'll read specific examples of how to go about it. You will learn what workout ideas best apply to you and your goals.

Time-Saving Training for Multisport Athletes will show you the most direct route to realizing your fitness potential.

TIME FOR TRAINING ADAPTATIONS

© Ken Lee

When triathlons first became popular early in the fabulous '80s, people jumped on the sport with the characteristic excessiveness of the decade. Stories abounded of job losses, divorces, and lost tri-geeks. Social worth in some circles was weighed in training mileage. Most of those people have either remained lost or remarried and gone back to work. Excessiveness doesn't work. Most of us who enjoy a fit lifestyle are not interested in overcoming the demons of a grueling event. Nor does an overwhelming training schedule hold much appeal. A successful exercise plan should enhance the rest of your life, not take away from it.

Multisport training has evolved into a healthy hobby for regular people who work and have families. Common sense will always prevail. It is the same whether you are a competitive triathlete or someone who simply enjoys those three modes of exercise and might occasionally enter some sort of event. If you don't earn your living at it, then you do it for fun. At best, training is a third priority.

There is much new information about how to train more efficiently. The sport of triathlon and multisport training have provided researchers with a whole new arena of investigation. Although exercise physiology is still a young science with much to learn, one conclusion keeps coming back. We can make substantial fitness gains from less time than we used to think necessary.

The effects of training are obvious. You can do more or go faster and you don't get as tired. Your fun factor gets a lift when these things occur. So the objective is combating fatigue. It's a big, ugly, multiheaded monster that has been able to hide a few of its noggins from science. The training system in this book takes aim at the heads that we know about.

There are some basics to help in understanding how this whole system works. The principles are supported by numerous and consistent studies. You're just going to have to trust me on the details, because we won't get into all that. There is nothing like a juicy research article to cure insomnia.

There are as many training responses as there are people. But there is one thing that applies to everyone. No matter what you want to do—run faster, juggle balls, cheat at cards—you need to practice that skill. Your body will respond to the training you give it. The response reflects the input. To go faster, you need to increase your training tempo. Increasing your pace for shorter distances will also generate pronounced fitness gains. Do less, gain more. It all sounds like a great deal. It works, but as we all know, there are no free rides. They ended in the fabulous '80s.

You need to learn to build up both the intensity of training and the time you train at higher levels. The key factor, however, is that time increases of only a few minutes transfer into big performance gains. Just like anything else, you can't do it all at once. That's good in a way, because it can give you years of continued improvement. I have a 50-year-old client with whom I have worked for four years. He trains less than he did five years ago but is steadily improving his triathlon times at all distances. He improved his marathon time by a half hour with three days a week of run training, and he is still

The end result of your training is that your events should be fun.

getting faster. His tolerance of higher level training increases each year.

With this type of training, you spend less time overall but more time going faster. Intensity base training works by building speed in small increments and working up. So the first element in saving time is building an intensity base. This will involve some adaptations in both your aerobic and your anaerobic systems.

It is not a matter of how much you train, but how you train.

ENERGY SYSTEMS

You have an aerobic and an anaerobic system to produce energy for exercise. One system, geared for short sprints, doesn't matter for endurance sports. A misconception is that you turn off one system and turn on another. It's not quite like that. At most efforts, you use a varying blend of both. Only very easy work is completely aerobic, and only all-out sprints of a few seconds are completely anaerobic. The rest is in between. The mixture depends on how fast you go and your fitness level.

The interaction between the two is an important element in raising fitness levels on limited time. Simply put, your aerobic system uses oxygen to produce energy, while the anaerobic system produces energy without oxygen. Muscles use the energy to pull on bones and produce movement. If you don't get tired, you can move your bones faster. That's about all there is to it. Some muscle fibers are able to use more oxygen than others. The maximal amount of oxygen that you can consume ($\dot{V}O_2$max) is simply a measurement of the amount of oxygen that your heart can deliver and your muscles can consume. So the desired training effect for endurance sports is a stronger heart and more aerobic-type muscles.

Your muscle composition plays a role in the fatigue monster's plans. Muscles are composed of different types of fibers, which you can alter through training. There are fast-twitch fibers, slow-twitch fibers, and those that lie in varying degrees between, which are the most important. All these fibers respond to the type of training that you do. Slow-twitch fibers have more endurance and are more aerobic in nature than fast-twitch fibers. Fast-twitch muscles are more powerful, don't need oxygen, but lack endurance. Genetics determines the original distribution of your fiber types. People who are gifted in endurance sports have a high percentage of slow-twitch fibers. Natural-born sprinters and people who excel in explosive movements have a higher percentage of fast-twitch fibers. Few of us, however, are a natural-born anything. Most are adaptable. All these kinds of fiber types and people who own them are just waiting to be trained. We aren't talking about Olympic medals, but about individual performance gains.

Most of your training adaptations will lie in the gray area between the aerobic and anaerobic systems. You have tremendous capacity to alter the performance capabilities of muscle fibers. So the fastest way to make fitness gains is to make changes in that adaptable area.

When you are working hard, you are using a delicate blend of both energy systems. You are recruiting both fast-twitch and slow-twitch muscles. Your primary fuel source is carbohydrates. The speed that you can maintain is dictated by the fiber types that you recruit to do the job. Endurance training changes fiber characteristics. At slower paces, we recruit slow-twitch muscles and use aerobic metabolism. As you begin to go faster, you recruit more fast-twitch fibers and blend in some anaerobic metabolism. If you slow down, the fast-twitch muscles get a rest and you shift back.

When you train in this blending state, the fast-twitch fibers that you recruit begin to take on slow-twitch qualities. That means that they can use oxygen to produce energy. Scientists argue whether the fibers change types or merely change in aerobic capabilities. When you get into the microscope it gets a little complicated. The result is that it becomes easier for you to go faster. You take on the ability to work at a higher level using aerobic metabolism. All that you need to do is regularly raise your muscle recruitment into this aerobic/anaerobic blending state.

You will often hear phrases like "I went anaerobic" or "I was in serious oxygen debt." There is no "debt." You don't run out of oxygen when you shift to anaerobic metabolism. You simply recruit more fast-twitch muscles and use more anaerobic metabolism. Lactic acid is a by-product that can accumulate, cause discomfort, and ultimately slow down muscle contraction. It is part of the process that makes us tired. It can also be a fuel source that keeps us from becoming tired. It is interesting stuff.

THRESHOLD TRAINING

Threshold can be an ambiguous term. There are several thresholds that people and researchers and magazine writers talk about. We need to identify just which one is most important. A common term is anaerobic threshold, or "AT." But remember, we don't just "go anaerobic." We change blending speeds. A second threshold is one at which breathing patterns change—the ventilatory threshold, or "VT." And there are two lactic acid thresholds. One marks the first appearance of lactic acid in the blood, which occurs during long-distance training at a comfortable pace. This corresponds to a perception of 11 on the Effort and Lactate Scale (see table 1.1). Studies have shown this to correspond with a concentration of blood lactate of 1, so we refer to that level as "L1."

The lactic acid threshold that is your pathway to time-efficient training parallels 16 on the Effort and Lactate Scale. It corresponds to a blood concentration of 4, and so is termed "L4." This is what we will call "lactate threshold," or "LT." This is the highest blood lactic acid concentration at which most people can exercise. The time that you can perform at this level is a function of training. If you are just starting out, it's about two minutes. As you become more fit, you can hold that level for longer periods. The reason for the time difference lies in threshold drift, which we get into in chapter 5. At lactate threshold and just under that level, there is a very delicate balance of lactic acid produced and consumed. This balance will differ among individuals concerning both training and genetics. Ventilatory threshold (VT) occurs at about the same work level as lactate threshold but is coincidental. When you

Table 1.1 — Effort and Lactate Scale

	Effort	% max heart rate	% $\dot{V}O_2$max	Blood lactate
19	Maximal	100%	100%	
18				
17	Very hard			
16		90%	87%	L4
15	Hard			
14		85%	80%	L2.5
13	Somewhat hard	80%	70%	L2
12				
11	Fairly light	70%	56%	L1
10				
9	Very light			
8				
7	Very, very light			

First two columns are based on Borg's RPE scale, 1985.

notice a breathing change and the work is getting hard, you know that you are in the threshold range.

Scientists have written that athletic people can hold a threshold work level for an hour. Theoretically this may be correct, but the researchers don't have to do it. A half hour is above average, and 10 minutes is doing well. There is a degree of discomfort at lactate threshold. Anything more is downright painful.

Training in the area from 14 to 16 is considered threshold training. But there is a difference in perception of effort between the two. When you are at a 14, there is still a degree of comfort. When you are at a 16 level, you are not comfortable. So most threshold training should put you at a 16 level only for a short time. You are training your muscles to work at faster paces aerobically. It is in this range where the most profound training adaptations take place.

As you adapt to going a little longer and a little faster in a threshold range, you also adapt to going a little faster at lower intensity. If you can run five seconds per mile faster at threshold, you can also run at least that much faster at an Ll

Learning to stay comfortable and relaxed on the bike will improve your performance with no additional training time.

level. This is how threshold training can transfer to performance at Ironman distance.

Threshold work is training the blender. The problem is what to do with the accumulation of lactic acid. You can feel its onset, and it can make your muscles feel like a brew of five-minute epoxy and lead. The solution is to use lactic acid as a fuel.

Untrained people have to stop when the epoxy starts to set up. But as you do more threshold training, muscle fibers adapt and begin to convert the lactic acid back to its original state as a fuel source. Chemically, the stuff is a carbohydrate, similar to sugar. It is produced when you go faster and begin to recruit more fast-twitch muscles. The more often you recruit these muscles, the more they begin to take on the characteristics of slow-twitch fibers. You will develop a higher percentage of lactate guzzlers relative to lactate producers. Trained muscles in your arms and legs begin to mimic heart muscle and are able to convert lactic acid to fuel just like the pump. Heart muscle loves the stuff. An accumulation of lactic acid in the blood means dinner time for the heart and trained muscles.

The more muscle fibers you change to having slow-twitch characteristics, the faster you can go. Because the lactic acid is being used as a fuel source, less of it is dumped off in your blood. You feel better and go faster. In essence, you raise your lactate threshold. The training to do these wonderful things inside your muscles doesn't involve much time.

In chapter 3 we'll look at how all this relates to your heart rate.

DISTANCE BASE

Training in the excessive '80s paralleled the viewpoint that more is better. That process increased distance first, and then added speed as the season progressed. The main idea was to improve your maximal aerobic capacity ($\dot{V}O_2$max) and increase fat-burning ability. However, slow distance training, like any other, is specific. You learn to go slow. Moreover, a sluggish pace for a long way takes a lot of time. Too much distance work and training time gave triathlon a bad reputation. It appeared to be just too much in all ways.

You need to build your aerobic capacity, but you can do it without '80s-style distance. You can better enhance both the strength of your heart and the ability of your muscles to use oxygen with short workouts. Many of these workouts take from 30 to 60 minutes. The importance of distance work lies in completing the event. So occasionally you need to sustain an easy effort for the amount of time that you expect to spend in your event. You don't need to do this year-round. Fat burning is not an issue for most people at race level, because their primary fuel source is carbohydrates. We'll get into the lard in chapter 9.

When you consider the time that swimming, cycling, and running have been around as individual sports, triathlon is still relatively new. Many of the training programs have been handed down from single-sport disciplines and simply combined to produce a new program. More important, these single-sport programs come from coaches of elite athletes. A common belief is that it worked for them, so it must work for everyone.

Elite athletes, however, are different. Many are so athletically gifted that they don't have to work regular jobs. Training is their job. Race day is payday. Because of the amount of training and racing and traveling in their jobs, they need time off. Anyone who has ever had any kind of a road job knows what I'm talking about. At the end of a racing season, a true pro is probably fairly tired. They may be gifted, but they are still human. To halt training completely is not a good idea, so they train less at lower intensity. They aren't really building anything. They are resting from a hard season and mentally preparing themselves for another one. They have also trained and raced very near their full potential. Further gains for them will be minimal. But the traditional work ethic still dictates that they put in a full week. The rest of us aren't looking for ways to fill a training week. Few are anywhere near full potential. Training and racing are a hobby—rest and recreation from the real work world.

Even under an intensity-based program, most people will never see the intensity or duration of the pros. If 10 percent of total time in a three-hour running week is in the threshold range, that's 18 minutes. Elite runners might put in 25 percent of their time at threshold in a 12-hour week, which is three hours. A normal person can do the 18 minutes on a year-round basis, and see continued improvement. But no one can take the three hours a week for more than a couple of months.

To get stronger you must steadily increase the load on your muscles. This is called overload. Anything that doesn't build on prior exercise is maintenance training. You can overload with more distance at a slow pace, or you can increase the intensity of a workout. You naturally want the most benefit with the least amount of time and lowest risk of injury. Research abounds with instances of training injuries linked to distance. Running is especially troublesome when an athlete lumps speed work or intervals on top of long, slow training. A common scenario is that an athlete becomes overtrained or sustains an overuse injury. The key word is overuse, but intensity gets the blame. The common conclusion is that there wasn't enough "base" building before the intervals. Of course, that depends on how you define base. Some people define base by the completion of a sometimes arbitrary amount of distance. Your base should be a measure of fitness rather than a distance log. You have a good fitness base if you are within 7 percent of your $\dot{V}O_2$max, or lactate threshold at a peak. My software program, Performance Progress Plus, can evaluate these levels for you. (For more information about the software, see page 180.)

More likely, the injured runner was on the brink of a problem during the distance-building period, and it was simply additional running that caused the problem. Total training time is the most likely culprit.

Recent studies from Germany address this issue. A consistent finding is that increasing distance brings on overtraining and a performance decline. Moreover, increasing intensity improves running performance significantly and brings on no

In a time crunch one big set can take a very short time and can be better training than the same amount of swimming broken into smaller sets.

overtraining symptoms. Quantifying just the right distance and intensity is still individual. The workouts in chapter 6 give some examples, but you will have to experiment. Most people find that they need to train much less than they thought. If you add hard interval work on top of increasing distance, you are inviting trouble.

INTENSITY BASE

To go faster you need to train faster. If you've been doing triathlons or regularly training in one of the three sports for a year or more, your maximal aerobic capacity is not likely to change more than the 7 percent mentioned previously. Over-distance training is not going to enhance it, and time off won't hurt it much. A study of swimmers showed that six weeks of no training had little effect on $\dot{V}O_2$max. That doesn't mean there is not a drop in performance. You can have a large drop in performance without a change in aerobic capacity. A period of easy training is not necessarily bad; it just puts your training on hold and doesn't build anything. But light training, a month off, or even a few months off, doesn't put you at a point of starting over. You will still have your base of aerobic capacity without worrying about building distance. Ideally, you will be able to build from one year to the next without starting over. You want your performance enhancement to be a year-round project. You can do this with the different phases outlined in chapter 4.

When you begin an exercise program, the first response is that your cardiovascular system gets stronger. Your heart pumps more blood with each beat, and the circulation to your muscles improves. Once these changes have oc-curred, they stay with you unless you quit all activity completely. But whether you are just beginning a training program, or have been at it for years, the same workouts will make the necessary changes. The cardiovascular system doesn't need a variety of training; it just responds to training demand before the muscles do. The effect is also longer lasting than changes made in your muscles. That is why the swimmers in the study mentioned above had no change in aerobic capacity.

You begin to build your intensity base by adding speed and power in small increments and increasing the time little by little. Distance training only gets your body accustomed to steady exercise for the amount of time that you expect to spend in your event. You can gradually add that time once you have noticed a fitness change from the higher intensity workouts. The first goal is to raise your threshold speed with only a minimal increase in your overall training time. This usually amounts to a matter of minutes in any one workout. That leaves you fresh for learning to go faster without the fatigue from continual distance training.

Even if you are just beginning, you can still begin with small amounts of training at a higher level. Higher intensity training will build your aerobic capacity more efficiently than distance. It takes less time and enhances the recovery process. I work with a 70-year-old semiretired bank executive who improved his aerobic capacity by 28 percent in his first three months. He has subsequently improved his holdings at about 5 percent per quarter. He works out on a stationary bike twice a week for a half hour when he isn't fishing. He does one- to three-minute repeats at 80 percent of his max heart rate, with equal amounts of rest, and occasional sprints with ample rest. The only real increase in his training is the power he puts out at that 80-percent level and the amount of time he spends there. His sessions on the bike are still a half hour or less.

Intervals aren't necessarily "speed" work. Don't make the mistake of going too fast when you are training at shorter distances. The pace needs to be only slightly faster than what you have been previously doing. If you have done nothing other than easy training, then all you need to do is spend short amounts of time in the "somewhat hard" range. You are in threshold training range when your effort reaches 14 on the Effort and Lactate Scale (see table 1.1) or your heart rate is above 80 percent of maximum. In fact, if you go too fast on some of the workouts, you can slow down the process. Workouts vary in intensity, which we will get into in the next chapter.

A key effect of building an intensity base is making the changes in muscle fibers that allow them to both convert lactic acid and use oxygen. If you never raise your level of exertion,

Many people will go out too hard early in the swim. It's easier if you save a little for later.

you won't recruit those extra fibers. They will remain lactate producers and won't consume oxygen. Your muscles will do only what is necessary, based on what you ask them to do. If you always go slowly, you will never recruit those additional muscle fibers. They go to work only when they have to. When you put them to work often enough, you can go faster and it's easier.

Even if you don't spend much time training, you can still build an endurance base with higher intensity. Once you have made a threshold change, you will find that distance work comes much easier. You can spend the winter just doing 30-minute workouts on a stationary bike three days a week and still go out and ride 50 miles when the weather gets warm. And you will do it a lot easier than if you had been doing regular, slow 20-mile rides in the rain and snow.

So rather than building distance and adding intensity, first build your intensity and add distance when you need it. Your ability to go longer distances will come much faster. The amount of distance depends on what kind of events you will do. If you plan on an Ironman, you will need to do some 100-mile rides and learn to run the amount of time that you expect in a marathon. You can build to those distances slowly, with the big ones a couple of months away from your event.

EFFECTS OF TRAINING WITH AN INTENSITY BASE

You will go faster and feel better. It will all come through the mechanisms that follow. Everyone is different, with natural strengths and weaknesses, but through one or more of these attributes you can begin to bite off the heads of the fatigue monster. For the most part, training effects are sport specific. So a change in one area may not affect the others. We'll note some of the exceptions, which can be very useful, in chapter 4.

Rise in $\dot{V}O_2$ Max

As $\dot{V}O_2$max increases, so does your overall work capacity. $\dot{V}O_2$max reflects the ability of the heart to pump oxygenated blood and the number of muscle fibers that can use the oxygen. It is measured in milliliters of oxygen used per kilogram of body weight. Most recreational athletes measure around 50 ml/kg, and elite athletes and pros are often in the 80 ml/kg range. If you were to run a mile as hard as you possibly can, you would be at max at the end. If your fastest all-out pace has risen from a 6:30 mile ($\dot{V}O_2$max 53) to a 6:15 mile, then your $\dot{V}O_2$max has increased to about 55. You could then run a 7:00 mile with less effort and sustain that pace for a longer period. A change in $\dot{V}O_2$max will also occur in swimming and cycling and cause the same effect.

Rise in Lactate Threshold

This would be a rise in the percentage of $\dot{V}O_2$max that you can sustain for at least two minutes and then repeat the effort a few times after short rests. Most performance gains in all three sports will occur as a result of changes in threshold. This is the area in which you have the most control. In swimming, if your time for 200-yard repeats has gone from 3:00 to 2:50, and the effort remains the same, then you have raised your threshold for swimming. Before you call the papers to announce this milestone, you should make sure that your effort hasn't increased with your faster times. A workout with greater than normal motivation can sometimes be construed as a fitness change. The mind can fool the body.

Threshold Drift

A pace that you can maintain for two minutes may not be sustainable for 10 or 20 minutes. In theory you can do it, but the real world says otherwise. As you continue a pace that is slightly under threshold, there is a slight upward drift in heart rate, oxygen consumption, lactate accumulation, and perceived effort (see figure 1.1). The graph shows only that oxygen consumption is rising, but everything else goes up as well. At the later stages, one of the training effects is to minimize this drift. A steep line indicates a considerable amount of drift and slowing of pace. A line more like the solid one in figure 1.1 will result in large time reductions in races. It's amazing how much time you can lose when your pace drops off even a little.

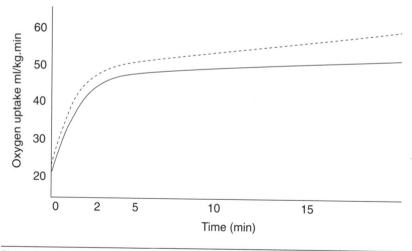

Figure 1.1 Oxygen consumption rises as pace is held slightly under threshold. This is called threshold drift.

RUNNING ECONOMY

Running economy is part form (see chapter 7), part muscle fiber recruitment, and part unknown. What is known is that you will use less oxygen at a given pace than you did before. That pace will feel easier. Running economy can help late in a race when inefficient runners begin to fade. It's sort of like two cars with the same-sized gas tanks going the same speed. The less economical one will run out of gas sooner. As you become more economical, you will delay running out of gas and finish more strongly. If you care about finish placing, this will become a more important consideration.

CYCLING POWER

Cycling power is measured in three ways: power at threshold, power at $\dot{V}O_2$max, and short-term sprint power. Someday, we will have bike computers that measure power. Speed doesn't tell us much unless we're on a flat with no wind. The actual work that you are doing is better measured by power, which is expressed in watts. In my research, I've found that people who have a very high power output for a half minute to two minutes can also perform well in a 20-mile time trial. I've also seen these results extend to half-Ironman and Ironman times. This amount of power is usually slightly greater than your power at $\dot{V}O_2$max, which would be all-out effort at the end of a 12- to 15-minute climb. Sprint power can be thought of as a power reserve. It is a larger amount than you normally use, but as it develops, big changes can take place in your long-distance cycling.

It is this power reserve that helps elite cyclists break some rules of physiology in the efforts that they maintain. Normal recreationally fit people have a ratio of around 1.1 to 1 of short-term (two-minute) power to the power that they can put out at $\dot{V}O_2$max. What this means is that if your power at $\dot{V}O_2$max is 300 watts, then your sprint power is 330 watts. You should do sprint workouts at this level. Elite racing cyclists are often well over 2 to 1. If we measure power alone, Tony Rominger, who now holds the hour distance record, has a $\dot{V}O_2$max of over 120. This is impossible. His true max is probably in the 80s. It is the huge amount of power reserve that allows him to maintain such a high degree of effort.

Even if your training does nothing to raise your $\dot{V}O_2$max or lactate threshold, if you can raise your power reserve, you will ride faster, farther, and easier.

FATIGUE (THE MONSTER)

So far, I have briefly talked about measurable differences that occur with a sound training program. All relate to fatigue. If we didn't become tired, we could go as fast as we want, for as long as we want. Unfortunately, the exact cause of fatigue remains unknown. There is a missing head to the monster. Fatigue is a combination of the preceding variables and more. Possible factors are speculation at this point. There are some things we do to fight the monster, but we aren't sure exactly why they work. So we do part of any type of training on faith.

We know that if you do certain things, you won't get as tired when you do them again. That is the essence of training response. We know that more training is not necessarily optimal. We can do more with less. An important element is that you work out at varying effort and distance. Any kind of training reduces fatigue. The more specific the training, the less time it takes.

TIME AT THRESHOLD: INTENSITY IS THE KEY

© Richard Etchberger

Achieving higher fitness levels, faster races, and less training time depends on training intensity. Like adding spices to your cooking, a little goes a long way. Just as you don't load up on the cayenne pepper and Tabasco if you have been on an oatmeal diet, you don't immediately jump into all-out speed work: Spicy food and intense training can both be hard on the system.

Your body needs a period of adjustment. When you add too much intensity too soon, you may not necessarily become injured, but you may develop other health problems like colds or flu. In chapter 3, we'll get into training and illness; the main point here is that hard training can be stressful if you aren't accustomed to it. Too much distance training can be even more stressful. Whenever you change your training schedule, you will have to pay close attention to signals from your body.

Training intensity means that you will train faster. Faster is usually harder. Anything that increases difficulty carries some stress. Stress is good to a point. However, periods of multiple stresses, which we all experience, often call for compromise. Job and family stress, along with diet and sleep, feed into the stress cycle. They can add to it or take it away, depending on the circumstances. Everything you do affects your training response. When one of these areas gets out of balance, something has to give somewhere. Job stress has a way of disrupting other areas. It can also lead to a lack of sleep, so you then have two factors that limit your training response. It's all part of life's balancing act. Everyone is different, but don't expect as much out of your training in difficult times. Keep well within your limits and use the training as a stress release.

GAUGING INTENSITY: HOW TO USE THE EFFORT AND LACTATE SCALE

The paces of harder training will vary widely among individuals. But the sense of effort is the same for everyone. The perception of "hard," or 15 on the Effort and Lactate Scale, is the same for Miguel Indurain as it is for the casual weekend rider. Miguel just rides a little faster. It is more important to remember that what you are feeling at any level of intensity will never change. The changes will be in what you are *doing* at those perceptions. You will be going faster and learning to hold an effort longer. There is a little Indurain lurking in all of us. Changes in heart rate will also occur, as we will see in the next chapter.

What you sense as you increase intensity is a buildup of blood lactic acid. You can feel even small increases in the concentration. Perception of effort correlates very highly with concentrations of blood lactate. This is good news, because lactate levels give us some realistic evaluations of exercise tolerance and fiber recruitment. An effort of "very light" indicates for everyone that mostly slow-twitch fibers are recruited. The faster you go, the more fast-twitch fibers you recruit and the more lactic acid you produce. But the only way to measure this whole process is to stick a catheter in your veins while you are exercising and then analyze your blood. Oh boy, now that sounds like fun! It's not something that you will want to do often, so depending on getting the information this way isn't of much use. You want your training progress to be continual, however, so you need a different method of continual monitoring.

Even if your perception of effort doesn't exactly match the correlating blood lactate acid concentrations in table 1.1, it will be close and can serve as a baseline performance evaluation.

TRAINING LEVELS

The levels described below define training intensity. The sample workouts in chapter 6 will refer to these stages in prescribing how hard to go.

L1. The first appearance of blood lactic acid is a concentration of 1. You are just beginning to sense that you are working. It is "fairly light," an 11 on the Effort and Lactate Scale. This is a distance and recovery effort. The sample workouts will show it as "L1." Your exercising muscles are warm, but the work is still quite comfortable.

L2. This ranks as, or corresponds to, a 13 on the Effort and Lactate Scale. It is "somewhat hard." You can definitely tell that your muscles are starting to work and recruiting some additional fibers. You can carry on a conversation, but you might be starting to cut your answers short.

L2.5. It may not make much sense to go up only a half notch, but the difference begins to become more noticeable right at this point. At 14 on the Effort and Lactate Scale, this effort is not quite "hard." There is still some degree of comfort, but you aren't quite the social animal that you left behind at L2. This level is just under lactate threshold, but from a training standpoint, it can be lumped together with L4. This is your most important range for making training adaptations.

L4. Lactic acid builds up more quickly after this point. Going just a little faster becomes a lot harder. Figure 2.1 shows how this changes with pace. You should do little if no training above this level. At 16 on the Effort and Lactate Scale, you will sense L4 as slightly more difficult than "hard." So you might feel a little cranky at this effort. Often, at this point, there is a change in your breathing pattern. In running, your breathing will follow some sort of footfall rhythm but will change at L4. A common threshold pattern is two steps per inhale and two

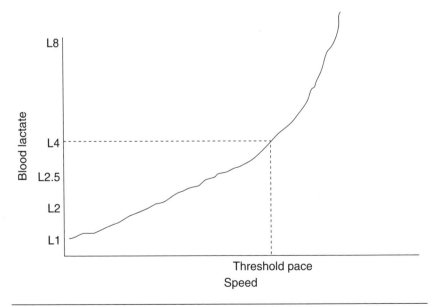

Figure 2.1 Lactic acid builds up quickly at an L4 training level.

steps per exhale. Your sense of humor will temporarily leave you. You have made a pH change in your blood, and initially your brain doesn't like it. Although it adapts over time, don't expect to be cheerful at threshold. That's why you don't spend much time there. We do this for fun.

The more you tune in to your perceptions of effort, the more you will be able to discern small changes or lack of change. The goal is to learn to work faster without a change in effort. You should be able to tolerate large percentages of time at a threshold level. But if you are at about a 12 level (just above L1) and raise your effort quickly to a 14 or 15, then your time at threshold will be much shorter. The good news is that in this state, just minutes of threshold training will work wonders.

If you can hold a 16, or L4, level for longer than 20 minutes without the effort climbing to an 18 or 19, you are very fit.

HOW HARD TO TRAIN

Simply put, the most profound training responses will occur when you train faster. How much faster, and how much time you spend at these faster paces will vary with your experience and fitness level.

What is actually accomplished regarding pace will be highly individual. I once worked with a nonrunner who wanted to become one. He had been doing regular weight training but no aerobic activity. I started him on quarter-mile repeats. Sounds too hard? That was as far as he could run—at any pace. It took him 3 minutes to run the distance at what began as perceived exertion of 12 and ended at 14. Then he rested for 3 minutes. We started out with three repeats and worked up to six. Sometimes he would do 30-second sprints. He loved those. His schedule gave him three days a month, at about 30 to 45 minutes per session, with 9 minutes of effort at L2 or above. In his case, an L2 effort would change to an L4 in about a minute. He also walked for a total of an hour per week. Within

Training with a group can often raise your training level.

a couple of months, he brought his quarter miles down to around 2:50 at a slightly easier effort level. This represents an 8 percent improvement in aerobic capacity. A total of an hour and a half per week, with less than 10 percent of his time at a higher intensity, did the job.

Another client was an experienced triathlete, admittedly of greater athletic talent than the nonrunner, but whose motivation is fun in training and racing in his age group. In a training week totaling nine hours, he responded well to work of about an hour of his time near threshold in swimming (36 percent), an hour running (20 percent), and an hour and a half cycling (33 percent). Of course, he did not do all this at once, but spread it out over the week. The rest of the time was at an L1 level. His previous training was 12 to 14 hours per week and fairly unstructured. Less total training time, but with an increase in threshold time, increased his potential an average of 5 percent in all three sports. This converts from a 2:02 for an international distance triathlon to a 1:57. At those paces, five minutes is a very big chunk of time.

Remember, threshold time is everything above a perception of 14 or L2.5. Once you go out and try it, you will find that there is a very big difference between a 14 and a 16. And it is in the lower ranges of threshold training where you will make the big gains. I'm not going to say that it's the same as lying in a hammock under a gently swaying palm, but there is some degree of comfort at a 14 effort.

Intensity above 16 (L4) is usually for shorter duration, and you get more rest between repeats. Do these workouts only once or twice a month, and only if you are highly competitive. At a 14 to 15 effort, one way to progress is to shorten the rest time. In effect, you create a harder workout, which will build fitness, and you have shortened the session.

It usually takes a couple of minutes for your heart rate to catch up to the level of work. So if your efforts are less than two minutes, heart rate is not a good gauge. You always want to use perception of effort as your first gauge. Then check your heart rate and pace. It is the combination of the three that really evaluates the quality of your workout. So the perfect workout doesn't mean going all-out. The ticket is to get close to threshold range but only for short periods. We can call it your improvement pace. If you have been doing only easy work, then an L2 effort is enough. It just has to be faster than you have been going.

You still get to go easy, interspersing easy workouts with the interval sessions. Easy work also occurs during interval sessions and during warm-up and cool-down. So when you add it all up, a beginner would want 5 to 10 percent of total training time at the improvement pace in cycling and running, and up to 20 percent in swimming. The remainder of the time is easy. As you become more fit, you change these percentages up to 30 percent in cycling and running, and 50 percent in swimming. The total training time doesn't need to change appreciably. More often, it can become less. You only need to learn to go faster before you go farther. As you approach race season or a key event, you will want to do your L1 distance workouts up to the time that you expect to spend in a race. It is best to build the distance gradually over a period of months.

Most interval sessions should leave you with energy to spare—feeling refreshed and energized. Often, people find they have more energy after workouts than before. All you need to do is keep progressing. This means that you need to add repeats, shorten the rest, or go a little faster. The most profound gains are taking place when you are doing all three. Faster people don't work any harder than slower ones; they just finish sooner.

Remember that although your workouts may look more difficult on paper as you progress, your training adaptations will keep the effort unchanged.

MUSCLE RECRUITMENT: THE HEART OF THE MATTER

In many ways, muscle recruitment is the central consideration in boosting training efficiency. You need to train only hard enough to recruit more muscle fibers than you have in the past. If you have never trained above an L1 level, small amounts of L2 training will recruit more fibers. If you have never been able to sustain an L4 level for more than two minutes, extending it to five minutes will recruit more fibers. Part of the performance loss from aging results from additional fibers sitting idle too long. This can lead to a slow deterioration of the nerves that fire them. If your nerves stay active, the aging process is of much less concern. The first of these muscle fibers and nerves to go are the fast-twitch fibers, and they are the ones that we need to call on to maximize the training response. Remember that the faster you go, the more fibers you recruit. The immediate response is dramatic if you are new to higher intensity training. You should begin to notice an increase in general strength and energy level.

This process also brings on added secretions of growth hormone. If there is such a thing as the fountain of youth, it is the pituitary gland, which delivers this magic stuff. When your levels go up, your immune system will be enhanced, your muscles will become stronger, and your training response and recovery process will be faster.

Overload and Maintenance

One reason why people who only train easy for long distances never get any faster is that they are in a continual maintenance program. Any workout that doesn't progress from an earlier fitness level is maintenance training. You won't lose any fitness with maintenance; you just won't gain any. It would be like always riding the same loop at the same effort and pace. An overload workout would be doing the loop faster or picking up your pace for one-minute intervals. Overload is simply doing more work than you have done before. It requires that you recruit additional muscle fibers. Muscles need constant

Practicing a time trial effort alone will raise your racing confidence.

stimulus to get stronger. If the stimulus is too weak, or too infrequent, further strength gains won't take place. Overload can be going longer than you have before, but going longer won't make you faster. It will teach you to maintain your training pace. Overloading through intensity saves training time and changes your performance level.

When you are overloading your muscles, you must also rest them. It is during rest that all those wonderful changes can take place. The training only provides the stimulus.

You need to know when to train and when to rest. By learning this you will save time. If you are ever in doubt, it is better to undertrain. We'll get more into overtraining in the next chapter, but you can lose months of fitness gains if you are seriously overtrained. Remember that the remedy for undertraining is overload, not more training time or miles.

One of the great things about multisport training (running, swimming, cycling) is that different sports use different muscle groups. So as long as you aren't doing all three every day, there is some built-in rest. The amount of rest needed will vary between individuals and between sports. In a very general sense, you want to allow a day between workouts in all three sports. That's the easiest way to look at it, and it will work. Occasionally there will be some exceptions. Sometimes, you can put hard swimming or cycling workouts on consecutive days, especially if you are in an improvement phase in one of those sports. The value of running on consecutive days is highly individual. No one should have hard running days back-to-back. For some people, extra run days help. Others will wear down. Some people respond better to two days between runs. Most people will benefit the most from extra running days on occasional weeks. Recovery running is an oxymoron, but you can have recovery workouts in cycling and swimming. These easy workouts don't need to have a structure beyond including about a half hour of movement at an L1 level or below. They are meant only to keep the blood flow going to a trained area, which can speed the recovery process after an especially hard workout. An easy spin on the bike for a half hour is often good the day after a race. Just remember that if you work too hard or too long, you will impede your recovery.

CALCULATING THRESHOLD AND TRACKING THE CHANGES

Once you have found a routine that fits your schedule, the real issue is progress. If you don't become more fit on reduced training time, then the system doesn't work. Because nothing succeeds like success, you need to know that changes are taking place.

You should have some sort of repeatable workout so you can check your time, effort, and heart rate.

You don't have to use heart rate, but it is useful information. If you don't use a heart rate monitor, but instead check your pulse, be aware of two points. The first is that when you stop your heart begins to recover. After 15 seconds, the heart rate usually doesn't correspond to the work that you have been doing. So you need to check it quickly. Immediately upon stopping, start counting for a 6-second period. Then multiply by 10 for beats per minute. Second, you should begin your count with "0"; otherwise, you will high by 10 beats. (At the time you begin your count, you are at 0, not 1.)

You should maintain the same effort level from one test to the next. No matter what your fitness level, you can always go faster if you are highly motivated and are willing to hurt. It's best if the efforts are just under threshold, in that "comfortably hard" area at an effort of 14, or L2.5. Your effort may drift up to 15 and 16, but start out with the intention of 14. A repeat effort of about two to five minutes with short rest provides a good threshold baseline. It is a better comparison to repeat the same general workout.

Practicing other strokes will improve your distance freestyle.

- Swim test—Three to five 150- or 200-yard (or meter) repeats, with 20 to 30 seconds of rest. Use the last repeat to determine your baseline evaluation.
- Cycling test—A long warm-up and then a 14 effort for five minutes on a flat section. On a stationary bike, you could use two to five two- or five-minute repeats, with about a minute of rest. Use the last effort as your base.
- Run test—Three to five half-mile or mile repeats with 45 to 60 seconds of rest. Like swimming, use the last effort as your base.

The preceding tests serve as good measures to use as Performance Progress Plus entries. There is a tendency to pick up the level on the last repeat. Try to keep your effort the same.

It usually takes three to five repeats to raise your heart rate to the level of your work. It should stabilize at that point. If you do your bike test on the road, you should ride at an L1, or 11, level for a half hour, and then go right into the five-minute section.

There is a trick to using a heart rate monitor in the pool. Don't wear the chest strap. (They usually slip to become belly button straps.) Lay it at the edge of the pool in shallow water. As soon as you come in, stand up and place it on your chest. You should get a reading in about three seconds. If it's longer than that, you will have to try again. Your heart rate should be dropping quickly when you stop, so more than three seconds will reflect some recovery.

Fitness improvements tend to come in three-week cycles. Once you have been actively training (or even regularly exercising) for a year or more, your biggest fitness improvement will come through changes in the percentage of your max at threshold. Most active people are around 80 to 85 percent. Elite athletes often reach 95 percent and higher.

This is one area where elite athletes don't really have an advantage over the rest of us. Almost anyone can raise a threshold into these ranges. For some yet unknown reason, masters athletes often will have higher thresholds than their younger counterparts.

You can think of your $\dot{V}O_2$max as your engine and threshold as the horsepower that you can squeeze out of it. The engine can be big or small. Whatever your engine size, it was largely determined at the factory. But, like a 1959 Cadillac, a big engine isn't necessarily fast. Efficiency all depends on the mechanic. To make the car go faster, you tinker around and change the horsepower without changing the engine. If you put a fuel injection system from the 1990s on the Caddie, its potential will take a big jump. Those who consider their bodies like large American automobiles from another era may be faster than they think.

It works this way. Let's say you do 200-meter swim repeats in 3:35. The first couple were at a 14 effort, but the third through fifth crept up to a 15 effort. Your pace slowed to 3:40, with a heart rate of 150 beats per minute. That would be the baseline to compare to a future workout. Performance Progress Plus will project your potential for a 1,500-meter open-water swim to be 27:10, and your threshold to be 85.8 percent of max. So for three weeks, you swim three days per week using some of the workouts suggested in chapter 6. Your total swimming time per week would be 2 hours and 20 minutes. After the three weeks you swim the 200s again. Your time on the last few repeats drops to a 3:28, still at a 15 effort, but with a small increase in heart rate to 152. This indicates a rise in threshold from 85.8 percent to 86.9 percent, and your potential for 1,500 meters improved a minute and a half to 25:40.

Without calculations, a threshold and performance potential increase can be noted by faster pace, slight elevation in heart rate, and no change in perceived exertion.

Similar changes in cycling and running can total up to an improvement of seven minutes in an international distance triathlon. You may not be able to continue to improve your performance by those amounts, but substantial gains can go much further that you might imagine.

Let's look at how $\dot{V}O_2$max and lactate threshold interact for a couple of hypothetical European bicycle riders. We'll call them Sven and Jean Claude. Sven has $\dot{V}O_2$max of 70. That's pretty high. It's sort of like having a high IQ. Natural talent. Jean Claude comes from more common stock, and has a $\dot{V}O_2$max of 60, which is good, but not Tour de France material. He is a worker, however, and can maintain a pace at 95 percent of his max. Sven is a dreamer and Schnapps drinker and blows up at 80 percent of his capacity, but he can ride all day at 78 percent, even with a hangover. All else being the same, smart money is on Jean Claude to win the race (Sven, 80 percent of 70 = 56 $\dot{V}O_2$; and Jean Claude, 95 percent of 60 = 57 $\dot{V}O_2$). Jean Claude's threshold is a greater percentage of his max. In theory, he can work at a higher level. (Oxygen consumption can be equated to work capacity.)

Back on the road, Sven and Jean Claude want to race about an hour to a beach town in southern Spain and look for girls. Sven uses his natural talent to pull into the lead while Jean Claude waits for Sven's inevitable fade. For the first 10 minutes or so, Sven maintains his lead. He has been doing only distance training for nine hours a week. His hangovers have held back his intensity. Jean Claude has been doing his workouts as discussed in chapter 6 and has cut his time to four hours per week. After another 5 minutes or so, Sven begins to slow as he is not clearing his lactic acid as quickly as he is producing it. Jean Claude has reached a steady state of production and clearance and is holding his pace. Sven can't keep the pace and hits the beach 2 minutes behind the Frenchman.

© Ken Lee

Some days you might only have time for a quick run at lunch.

BEGINNING THE INTENSITY BASE

One day a week in whatever sport you want to improve should have some pace-building intervals. In swimming, I like to use 50-yard or 50-meter repeats with short rest as the speed base. The pace is slightly faster than if you were to go for 200. The beginners in my masters group always start with 50s and work up to 100s and so on. You then learn to hold your 50 pace for 100, and your 100 for 150 and up to 200. Of course, once you have taken a 50 pace and worked up to a 200, you probably have a new, faster 50 pace. A new carrot. This will also hold true with your 20-second or 60-second power on the bike and your 200-meter running time. Carrots are cheap and plentiful. You can take the progression as far as you want, or up to the limit of your genetic capabilities.

In cycling, short-term power is a big consideration in performance. You can build this with high-intensity intervals of 20 seconds and threshold intensity (L4) of at least a minute. The 20-second repeats allow you to build the neural component of cycling power. With an increase in power, you gradually raise your threshold for longer durations. You then adapt to extend a level that you can repeat for one-minute intervals up to two minutes. As you work into race season, try to work at a slightly lower level than that level during another session up to 20 minutes. Once you've done that try working up to 30 minutes. You will find some mental relief if you back off a little for about a minute, every five minutes.

In running, I use 200s and 400s to build speed, varying the workouts with both short and long rests. Run at a slightly slower pace to a half mile, then a mile. Work your faster paces into 10-minute runs and finally into 20-minute sustained runs on a different day than the short workouts.

Once you've raised your threshold, increasing distance will then come much faster and easier. Even if your goals include an Ironman, you can add the distance later. It's true that we all have limits. But even an old Cadillac can get faster with some new ideas.

TIME TO PREVENT TRAINING LOSSES

© Richard Etchberger

You can't create time. There are no 25-hour days. Saving time only cuts your losses. You can keep these losses to a minimum for both the long and short term. Short-term savings are obvious. You gain more training benefit from shorter workouts. Long-term savings insure that your training response remains high. If you don't respond to training, then time spent gains you nothing: It's wheel-spinning in the classic sense.

Your workouts are only half of the process. The more important half is recovery. Training adaptations take place when you are resting, not while you're training. Training only provides the stimulus. The time it takes to make the changes is your recovery, a process that can vary quite a lot. Some days your body responds better than others. You will have natural up and down cycles. You can't predict them, but you know when you are in a good one. When you're in a bad cycle, the natural tendency is to deny it. You need to be honest with yourself, and overcome that unbounded training lust. Part of effective training is learning to recognize down times and take advantage of the better ones. Good cycles are the times to do a little extra. If your response is strong, gains will come quickly. Fitness gains will always come in a stepwise fashion. So you want to get the most from an up cycle and maintain fitness when you plateau. Your improvement graph will never be a continual upward-sloping line. You will make life easier by learning to flow with these patterns. Fighting them is swimming against the tide.

When you experience a down cycle, backing off will help. Unfortunately, down periods are out of our control to a degree. Stress and outside influences also seem to come in cycles inconvenient to a training schedule. You shouldn't minimize the effects of job stress, family time constraints, lack of sleep, or changes in daily routine. You will perform very differently when your life runs in order than when it runs the fire drill that it can sometimes become. The training tolerance of trial lawyers seems to be inversely related to their court time and the complexity of their cases. When you perform poorly, the first response is to think that you aren't training enough. Possibly that's true, but you might be incapable of any more training. Sometimes your body is just the messenger you need.

You can only take so much. While your body seems to make adjustments for its surroundings and influences, the brain can be a stubborn tool that pushes you relentlessly.

It's all workable as long as you adapt. It always seems like a disaster while you're in a down phase, but you will bounce back quickly as long as you don't quit entirely. If you need a quick lift, it's amazing what you can do in the quick-and-dirty crash-training program outlined in the last chapter.

Usually you will need to train less when outside stresses grow.

Before we get more specific about the signs to watch for, know that you can save yourself much down time and disappointment by observing the old phrase "Listen to your body." It was probably a cave-dwelling shaman who said it first, but the maxim will always apply. The stubborn brain knows only to push on. It can make a slave of your body if you let it.

HEARTBEAT

How often your pump beats is an indicator of your exercise level. But looking at heart rate alone can be misleading. You need to look at heart rate along with how fast you are going and perceived effort. Together these three items can give you a tremendous amount of information. You can know if you are overtraining, undertraining, or making fitness improvements. You can also establish if you are running out of carbohydrate stores (glycogen), if you are dehydrated, or if you are heat stressed. Knowing these conditions will tell you if your training is on track.

Two methods people used in the past to gauge heart rates now are seen as largely ineffective. The first is estimating your maximum heart rate by age: No matter how you subtract or add or factor in anything, all these formulas still work on the assumption that your maximum heart rate will drop as you age. Although there is a tendency for a person's maximal heart

Make the most of your training time on a group ride, by meeting them out on the road, rather than driving to a gathering place.

rate to drop, that measure is highly individual and definitely doesn't decline a beat each year. People who have had little activity during their younger years and have become more active in their 50s sometimes experience a rise in their maximal heart rates. The other ineffective heart rate gauge is comparing yours with anyone else's. We are all different, and the only heart rate appropriate for comparison is your own at different times.

The standard that you should look at is a change in your heart rate at a given work level. This would mean running pace, swimming pace, cycling speed, or power output. The first thing to do is to establish a heart rate at a given exertion level. Table 1.1 gives a guideline about rough percentages of max heart rate. Let's use running as an example. You are running at L2, "somewhat hard." Your heart rate after 15 minutes at this level

Table 3.1 — Training Response Indicators

Run	Pace	Heart rate	RPE	What it means
First run	7:30	150	13	Baseline
Second run	7:40	145	14	Overtrained, ill, stressed, etc.
Second run	7:30	150	13	Training in maintenance
Second run	7:20	155	13	Threshold raised
Second run	7:30	145	12	Threshold raised

is 150 beats per minute. By the miles or quarter miles that you have marked out on your running route, you check your pace. You are going at 7:30 per mile. As your fitness changes over a few weeks, you might notice two things. You may have a slight rise in your heart rate to about 152 and an increase in speed to about a 7:20 pace, while still at L2. Or when you run a 7:30 pace, your perceived effort drops to a 12 and your heart rate dips to 145. Both scenarios demonstrate a rise in threshold and performance ability.

---

*M*ark out quarter miles on a bike path or road with your bike computer. Use a chalk mark, spray paint, or a landmark. Use these for doing run intervals instead of going to the track.

An increase in performance is great. Of course, it also goes the other way. A classic symptom of the early stages of overtraining or overall fatigue from any source is a rise in perceived exertion with the inability to raise your heart rate or pace. Whatever the reason, your training response will be minimized and you are wasting time trying. The best way to train on a day like that is to forget it. Now there is a real time saving. The chart in table 3.1 outlines a few scenarios for running: "First run" is a starting point and the rows labeled "Second run" show various possibilities for subsequent workouts.

At threshold, a common percentage of max heart rate is 85 to 92 percent. Effective training is creating a rise in this percentage. If you don't know your maximum heart rate, one way to calculate it is to take your threshold heart rate and divide it by 0.9 to get your max. At an effort of 16 on the Effort and Lactate Scale (L4) and a heart rate of 165, divide 165 by 0.9 to get 183 as a max heart rate ($165 \div 0.9 = 183$). This is usually much closer to a true max heart rate than a formula using age or resting heart rate. Whether or not that is your exact maximum heart rate is not as important as being aware of changes at given perceptions.

Your true maximum heart rate is that elicited by running. Highly fit cyclists who don't run are an exception. So your corresponding heart rates in cycling and swimming will be lower. Generally, cycling heart rates will be about 5 beats lower than running heart rates, and swimming heart rates will be about 10 beats less (see table 3.2). Everyone will vary from these numbers to a degree, and the paces are hypothetical, but the overall trend between sports will remain similar. If you want to know your true maximum heart rate, running up a hill that takes about 3 minutes at an all-out effort should get you to max. You need to have been running for about 15 minutes beforehand and at an L2 level for about 5 minutes before you start the hill. You will be glad when it's over.

Once you establish your heart rates at the different levels, you will need to keep in mind that it takes your heart two minutes to catch up to the work. If you are doing short intervals at a threshold level by perception, your heart rate might show a little low. Just remember that if you held that

Table 3.2 — Paces, Lactate Levels on Heart Rate

	L1	L2	L2.5	L4	Max
Swimming Hr:	125	140	150	160	179
pace/100 yd	1:39	1:35	1:31	1:28	1:21
Cycling Hr:	132	145	155	165	189
power	179 watts	221 watts	262 watts	276 watts	323 watts
speed	19.5 mph	21.1 mph	22.9 mph	23.6 mph	27.6 mph
Run Hr:	132	151	160	170	189
pace/mi	7:48	6:42	6:24	6:10	5:18

effort it would catch up. However, if you are overtrained or overreaching, your heart rate may not rise as it should.

Changes in the Heat

When you train in the heat, your heart rate response will be different. A part of what happens is that your body cools itself by diverting blood to the skin. Less blood goes to the working muscles so the heart beats faster to compensate. But it's not a full compensation. Blood is like money. There is only so much to go around, and everyone wants more. You have only five or six liters of blood, and your skin and muscles want seven. You can think of heat like a blood shortage. The result is that you produce more lactic acid, your clearing rate goes down, you use more carbohydrates (fuel), and you use more energy. Even at this higher price you will go the same pace or slower. When training in the heat you also run the risk of dehydration, which exaggerates all of this. It may be slightly less pronounced in cycling than running because of the effect of wind cooling, unless you can run comfortably at 20 miles per hour. If your heart rate rises more than 10 beats per minute at a given perceived effort, you are becoming dehydrated. The first thing to do is drink whatever is available. Sports drinks can hydrate you faster than water.

You may find that both your perceived effort and heart rate go up and your performance suffers. Look for numbers about 10 beats higher than normal at a given level of effort and a 5 to 10 percent decline in performance (speed).

Fuel Problems

During longer workouts or races you might encounter a heart rate response opposite that of the preceding scenario. If you begin to run out of carbohydrate stores (muscle glycogen), you may find a drop in your heart rate at any given effort level. This will accompany a decline in speed. Without taking in carbohydrates most people run out (bonk, hit the wall, etc.) in about two hours. You will have the sensation that you can't raise your heart rate no matter how hard you try. The first thing to do is eat or take in a fluid replacement drink.

In a long training session or race in the heat, you can become dehydrated, overheated, and glycogen depleted. That is just about the end of the fun. But you can head off trouble by paying attention to your perceived effort, pace, and heart rate early on to take care of trouble before it occurs. Recovery from a depleted workout takes longer and slows your training progress. An important way to keep your glycogen stores up is to eat some carbohydrates within a half hour of completing a workout. A couple of bagels and sports drink or juice will make a difference. If you wait more than a half hour, the process of building stores in the muscles is much slower.

Overreaching and Overtraining

Your heart rate can also tell you about your long-term response. You have four options for training load: optimal, over-training, undertraining, and overreaching, a newer term. Your training is optimal if you are continually getting faster and feeling strong and energized. Make a note of what works, but be watchful.

Treat chronic overtraining as an illness. Much research has been done in this area, and most of it is fairly consistent. You can monitor these classic symptoms:

- An increase of more than five beats per minute in resting heart rate
- Depression or irritability
- Inability to sleep
- Reduced training performance and desire to train
- Reduced appetite
- Weight loss
- Extreme muscle soreness

Overall, an overtrained person simply feels stale and sluggish and is on the edge of getting sick or is sick. Many overtrained people are walking around with low-grade infections that don't go away. People who have overtrained for a long

© Ken Lee

In the early days when few competitors wore wetsuits, hypothermia was a big problem in colder swims.

period experience these symptoms for weeks or even months at a time. Doing too many miles in too short a time is often the cause.

If you have blood drawn you might find (1) altered white blood cell count (lower immune response), (2) destruction of red blood cells (oxygen-carrying capacity reduced), (3) rise in cortisol (a stress hormone), (4) elevated muscle cell enzymes in the circulation (indicates muscle damage), or (5) fall in testosterone levels (good for population control). These conditions all affect your enjoyment of the sport and your life in general.

Overtraining damages the very things that we are trying to strengthen—the muscle cells. Overtraining impairs the membranes that surround the cell, which causes things to leak out, and damages the energy-producing mechanisms. A cell in disrepair requires as long as eight weeks to get itself back to normal. A marathon run will generally put you in this state. Fatigue lasting longer than a few days is definitely an indication. Muscle soreness is also a sign that damage has occurred.

The workouts just aren't doing any good. Along with a general suppressed immune response, overtrained people are likely to be sick. White blood cell counts will often be altered, red blood cells destroyed, cortisol levels increased, and testosterone levels decreased. You will be a shadow of your former self.

Overreaching, a new word coined by researchers, is different from long-term overtraining. It is the first indication of a lack of recovery and is usually not a serious problem. Recovery usually takes only a couple of days, up to two weeks at most. You might experience a rise in perceived exertion with no accompanying rise in pace or heart rate. Your workout feels hard and you are going slow. The earlier you catch this, the better. Some people can just go home and try the same workout the next day and everything is fine. You can think of this kind of fatigue as a protective mechanism. If you fight through it, you begin the process of long-term damage and overtraining. If you take a day or two off, you will heal and get stronger. If you want to improve your performance, you may get to an overreaching state fairly often. You have asked a little more than your body can provide. You have pushed the envelope, but haven't broken it. The time to back off is when you first notice the fatigue.

UNDERTRAINING

It is always better to err on the side of doing too little. You will feel a whole lot better, and people will like you more. (Overtrained people are grumpy.) And if you find that there is no progress, all you have to do is train a little harder. Or, if you are happy with your performance level, you might be able to undertrain slightly and maintain. You won't lose any fitness; you just won't get faster. If you are allowing more than four days between workouts in any one sport, you aren't likely to make much progress. Muscles need constant stimulus to get stronger. If the stimulus is too weak, or infrequent, further strength gains won't take place. You may at some point reach a training plateau. You then have to decide how important it is to go to the next step. The higher your fitness level, the more difficult it becomes to improve.

I know a professional triathlete who swims about 6,000 meters per week and comes in about a minute behind the guys who swim 15,000 to 20,000 meters per week. He has to decide how badly he wants that minute.

TRAINING AND ILLNESS

Several recent research studies have looked at exercise and its effects on the immune system. This work reminds us that training is a whole-body response rather than just muscle adaptation. Overtrained people have depressed immune systems. Most of what is being learned is making it easier for us to make training decisions. Good training decisions save training time.

Even though you must address specific muscles, your whole body is involved. Research findings give us good news but also some warnings. Probably no group of athletes is more fit than Tour de France riders. As the race progresses, however, many of them get as sick as dogs and drop out. You may have heard tales about other elite athletes coming down with a cold or flu just before a major event. Maybe it's happened to you. And you probably know someone who trains every day and hasn't had a cold in years. Some people never get sick. Reasons for these inconsistencies probably come down to distance and overall stress.

In essence, the immune system is composed of various white blood cells, which are manufactured in bone marrow, the spleen, and the thymus gland. The whole idea is to combat intruders (bacteria, viruses, fungi, allergens). The system comprises two categories, specific and nonspecific. The nonspecific part is like a hired thug who wanders around and kills on sight anything that doesn't belong. This thug also lends a hand in recovering from a hard workout by cleaning up cellular damage.

Specific immunity is a little more sophisticated. A system of antibodies communicates between immune cells to recognize a specific illness. You never get the same cold twice. But there

A regular schedule with consecutive run days at a moderate effort wastes time. Train with a friend to help you stick to a hard run every two days.

are over two hundred known cold and flu viruses (and probably more unknown), which is why we still get them.

The good news is that regular exercise enhances your immune system. But if you've ever come down with a cold or flu just after a hard training session, race, or stressful situation, you know that it's not quite that clear-cut. The culprit may be cortisol, a stress hormone. Some recent investigations are showing that depressed immune systems are associated with elevated levels of cortisol and other stress-related hormones.

Poor drivers in front of you in traffic, stress before races, idiot bosses or clients, and other assorted fools can all raise your cortisol levels. Everything can be going fine in training. Then an outside factor raises your stress level, and wham, you've got a cold. It seems like everything you've done up to that point just went straight down the toilet.

Dr. David Nieman has looked at marathon runners, moderate exercisers, and people who don't exercise at all. A key element lies in the definition of "moderate," which can vary tremendously between individuals. What constitutes "hard" training is really a combination of intensity and distance. Nieman has found a higher incidence of upper respiratory infections among the nonexercisers and marathoners than the moderate exercisers.

A recent study from Australia has shown that cyclists training 300 to 500 miles a week had depressed immune systems similar to the group of marathon runners in Nieman's work.

The root of the problem could be distance. Tour de France riders, marathon runners, and other high-mileage cyclists are all doing a lot of hard training. There is evidence to indicate that it is not so much the hard training, but the amount of it. In runners anyway, it appears that 60 miles per week is the point at which an immune system can break down. A marathon itself can be enough. A study in England recently showed that a marathon affected immune systems while an 18-mile run or a six-second sprint didn't. Anyone who has run a marathon knows all too well the difference in difficulty between 18 and 26 miles.

On the other side, studies are beginning to point out that short-duration efforts of high intensity could heighten immune response. Higher intensity training also stimulates the production of growth hormone, which builds both the immune system and muscles. An interval session of an hour with repeats in the L2 to L2.5 range should be beneficial for most people. Some people thrive on lots of threshold work at L4. The important thing is to stay within your level of tolerance.

Most exercise bouts of any intensity involve a rise in immunity during the exercise and a temporary depression immediately following. It can last for an hour up to a day. So if you train long and hard every day, you are walking around in a continually depressed immune state. Also remember that the immune system assists in recovery from exercise. So besides opening up your chances for an illness, you are also slowing down the muscle repair process. You begin to lose traction.

Prevent the Problems

Pay attention to the early signs of a sore throat and training staleness, indicators of trouble in the works. Overreaching symptoms are the beginnings of an immune depression.

If you are getting a cold from the neck up, back off early. You can maintain fitness on half of your regular training. Use a margin of error and don't train over L2 until the cold is gone. Once you have a fever and muscle aches, the virus is everywhere, including your muscles. At that point, training only enhances the strength of the bug. Nieman recommends two weeks to a month off. It might be good advice, but I have yet to meet the triathlete willing to do that.

Muscle soreness indicates that your immune system is working harder, so your susceptibility to an infection might be higher during these times. You are asking double duty from your immune system and it may, or may not, be up to the task. You need to rest the muscles that are sore and your body in general.

It all boils down to recovery. Some people need more than others. One full day of rest each week helps keep you honest. Most people can't go longer than three weeks of building before they need an easy week. Some simply need to alternate hard and easy weeks. That will also vary within individuals. Age, too, is a factor. Past the age of 35, most people begin to notice that recovery requires more time. If you aren't recovering, then you are overtraining. If you are overtrained, your immune system isn't working to full capacity.

CARBOHYDRATES AND TRAINING

Unless you are walking, your primary fuel for exercise is carbohydrates. You have blood sugar, and you have glycogen stored in the muscles and liver. Fat stores contribute to the total energy picture, but remain a minor player. For your workouts to have an impact on fitness, you need to keep your carbohydrate stores up. If you don't recover from a workout, then the next one won't be as efficient.

You have approximately 2,000 calories worth of stored carbohydrates. This will keep you going for a little over two hours. Most is stored as glycogen in the muscles that you train. You store more in trained muscles than in untrained ones. Muscle contraction is dependent on carbohydrates. When you run out, you slow down. It gets ugly. So you need to take in some form of carbohydrates during your longer workouts. This will keep you from running out of the precious stuff, keep you going, and help your recovery. Energy bars or sports drinks work equally well. It takes you longer to recover from workouts once you have become carbohydrate depleted.

Even if you do keep your carbohydrate stores up during your workouts, you should take in some carbohydrates immediately afterward, the sooner the better. By consuming carbohydrates during the first 15 to 30 minutes, you will be ready to train the next day or get efficient rest if you don't.

You can optimize your glycogen resynthesis if you take in two grams of carbohydrates per kilogram of body weight within two hours of your workout. This is a couple of bagels, some juice, and a piece of fruit.

It has been thought that a part of the overtraining syndrome was related to glycogen depletion. Studies have demonstrated that cyclists can adequately stock themselves with carbohydrate fuel yet still overtrain. So don't think that as long as you keep piling on the carbs you won't overtrain. Fatigue is still not that clear-cut. There are other things going on to make you tired. Remember that the fatigue monster has a number of ugly heads.

PROTEIN REQUIREMENTS

Carbohydrates are your fuel source, but your body is built of proteins and is in a constant state of breaking down and building back. It's one big urban redevelopment project. People on high-carbohydrate diets tend to get smug about their purity, but they may be accomplishing only the tearing down part of redevelopment. Carbohydrates are your main

It has never been a problem remembering that we do this all for fun.

source of energy fuel, but don't get carried away. A diet with caloric intake of carbs exceeding 60 percent is not better. You should take in 20 percent in protein, and 20 percent fat will come without even thinking about it. So it all adds up to 60 percent carbohydrates, 20 percent protein, and 20 percent fat.

Unlike fats and carbohydrates, there is no storage form of protein in the body. Proteins are composed of amino acids, some that your body manufactures, and some that you have to eat. Even though the carbs are the main fuel, protein accounts for about 3 to 5 percent of your energy. If you are short on dietary protein, you will go 3 to 5 percent slower and impair your recovery process. So another way of maximizing your training time is keeping the building materials in your diet. Researchers agree that athletes or active people need more protein than those who favor the couch life. They have established between 1.2 and 2 grams of protein per kilogram of body weight per day. Most people would get enough with a couple glasses of milk, four to six ounces of meat or poultry, a potato, and maybe some beans. If you are a vegetarian, you can get enough from nonanimal sources, but it's tricky. Animal proteins are complete with all the amino acids that you need. When you get your protein from other sources, you just need to remember that you only build to the amino acid of shortest supply. It's like a bicycle shop that has an order for 20 new bikes. The shop receives a shipment of parts that looks like enough for 20 bikes. But when they go to build the bikes, they find only 5 sets of handlebars. The rest of the parts go unused.

One of the biggest time wastes is a regular schedule with consecutive run days at a moderate effort. Eliminating some of these runs will cut back time and probably increase fitness.

SUGGESTIONS FOR TRAINING

Some basics:

1. Choose one day a week when you do no training or extremely light training.
2. Recovery from hard running workouts takes longer than recovery from cycling or swimming. This is especially true if your training involves any downhill running, which generates a tremendous amount of impact with each footfall. Depending on your recovery rate, sometimes it's better to let two or even three days go between hard runs.
3. In a general sense, you shouldn't do consecutive days of hard training in any of the sports, although occasionally it won't hurt to try it with cycling or swimming. Do this only if you have no overreaching symptoms, your progress is stalled, and you want to go to the next step.

4. You can't get any training benefit if you have extremely sore muscles. A little occasional tightness is all right. But watch out—muscle tightness is an early sign of over-reaching.

5. If your training isn't progressing, change something. You need either more recovery or less, either more intensity or less.

6. Each sport is specific concerning improvement. Mild overreaching can also be sport specific. So, if you have overreached running, you still might be able to put in a good swim workout. Overtraining involves your whole body, and everything you do is garbage.

7. You need easy days and easy weeks of training. Most people can build no longer than three weeks before they need a break. Sometimes it's every other week. Everyone is different, and everyone has varying cycles within themselves. Three weeks is the standard maximum for a building period.

4

TIMING PEAK FITNESS: THE SEASON PLAN

We've talked about different influences on training response that will help save time. Of course, all of this should lead to a pleasing conclusion of the perfect yearly training schedule. It begins in January and has you at your all-time peak for your key event on August 27. You can do that to a degree, but August 27 could be an off day for you. It happens. There is no perfect training schedule. Each of us has different needs and responses, and as we said in the last chapter, the responses can change. The needs usually remain the same.

We all have various gifts and shortcomings. Our gifts are something that we can rely on in a pinch. Our shortcomings need work. There are times in the year where you want to put an emphasis on one of the three sports. If you have a weakness, a couple of months of concentration will make a difference.

BASICS OF FITNESS CHANGE

It's easier to build speed early in the year, with a rotation of emphasis among the three sports. You build fitness in one area while maintaining in others. The best way is to alternate sports, paying the most attention to your weak one. But most people resist that. We tend to gravitate toward areas of greater skill or strength. No one wants to do what they don't do well. But with some work, weaknesses can become strengths. As you become stronger in an area, you will like it more. Call me an optimist. It could happen.

There are some basics to sport rotation. The first is that fitness gains tend to come in three-week cycles. Then a week of lighter training will get you ready to build again. Most researchers, old coaches, and storytellers will agree with this, although no one can tell you why. This is one of those points that you have to take on faith. It's a handy principle to use, in both the long and short term. You can do a crash cycle a month before a race if you've missed training (see chapter 9). You can also do a few cycles to strengthen a weak sport or strengthen your strong sport. A cycle consists of a three-week build period followed by a week of recovery or maintenance.

A second point to remember is that most people can maintain fitness in a sport by training two days per week (up to a point).

I'm taking a little latitude with this one. I've seen a two-days-per-week program bring improvement, maintenance, and a decline. An elite athlete in peak fitness might lose a little with two days. Someone starting out, or starting over, is likely to see improvement. For those improving, two days will probably bring an early plateau. But it may be a plateau that fits in nicely with your race goals. In that case, don't mess with success. You may want to stay on a year-round schedule like that. Generally, you can maintain a level of fitness on half the work that it took you to reach it. Improvement takes extra effort. Maintenance is easy. Human minds and bodies resist change. All of these sports will benefit from a time devoted to making single-sport fitness changes. Think of yourself as a swimmer for a time, a runner for a time, and a cyclist for a time.

The off-season can also be a good time to work on what you like. Many people get a little burned out if they have raced or trained a lot during the season. Doing what you want to do can be more of a mental break than doing nothing at all. So if you like to swim, then just swim for a while. You will always put a little more effort into something that you like. Even if you improve a strength, you are getting faster and more fit. Whether you concentrate on a strength or a weakness, taking the three sports one at a time will benefit you in the big picture.

The key to following these principles is sport rotation. You still need to maintain fitness in the sports that you're not trying to improve. You should work out two days a week (occasionally you can get by with one) with your maintenance sports. Maintenance means that you keep the same intensity that you trained with before. You cut back on time. If, in peak fitness, you could do 1-minute repeats on a stationary bike at 270 watts, you still need to do 270-watt repeats. You don't need to do as many of them and you don't need to do them as often. You can reduce the total time per week considerably by keeping two sports in maintenance.

SPORT ROTATION

The weather helps you to decide how to set up your rotation. In most regions, fall lends itself to running. Because the environment in the pool is constant, midwinter is a good time to maximize swimming. Spring is good for cycling as the roads begin to warm up and dry out. You don't have to set up your rotation in that order, but you want to give yourself two improvement cycles to make a change. A typical improvement cycle would have three weeks of building with a week of recovery. Two cycles would take two months. So equal improvement phases in all three sports will take six months. If

Taking splits during races helps to track performance changes.

you start in November, by the end of April you will be ready to go into a balanced phase of training.

This all sounds pleasant and tidy. Now let's look at the truth. Most people won't be able to stick to the plan. You'll be at the time when you are supposed to start your bike phase, and you just finished a run phase, but you still need a swim phase. Something will be off. It happens. Try to do at least two four-week cycles of your weakest sport. You know that the bike leg of a race is where you can make up or lose the most time. Most people will spend approximately half of their total race time turning pedals. The good news is that fitness changes tend to come quicker with cycling. Get your swimming and running in relatively good shape first. Some people can make big changes in a month of concentrated cycling.

No matter how good a runner you are, you won't perform to your potential in a race if you lack bike fitness. In an international distance race, you shouldn't drop by more than 10 percent of your fresh running. If you can run a 40-minute 10K, you shouldn't be any slower than 44 minutes in a triathlon. We get into this more in chapter 9. Unfortunately, the lower your fitness level, the longer the bike leg will take and the more fatigued you will be. Poor bike fitness can snowball in both directions during a race. If you get off the bike tired, your run can deteriorate to a slow motion movie. It's easy to lose as much as 5 minutes over a 10K. If you can ride 5 minutes faster and come off fresh, you will be able to run to your potential. It's easy to make up or lose as much as 10 minutes in an international distance race. You want your cycling fitness to be on an upswing as you begin racing.

You may find during a phase that you improve in a maintenance sport along with the sport that you are emphasizing. I worked with one athlete who, during a swim phase, began running better than he ever had on two days per week. If you maintain some degree of intensity, the extra rest may allow improvement. The key is that you are getting more rest in the sports that you are maintaining. This will help in long-term recovery in those sports and keep you fresh for the area that you are trying to improve.

IMPROVEMENT PHASES

Because you work hard to achieve fitness gains, you want to be sure not to lose too much in a maintenance sport. If possible, you don't want more than four days to pass between workouts. When you are in an improvement phase, you want to think of yourself as a single-sport athlete in your improvement sport.

Be a Swimmer

Most of the people in the masters swim group that I coach are triathletes. Some of them run beforehand. You ought to hear them whine about being tired from running and about the leg cramps. They greet a kick set with the enthusiasm of a sailor sentenced to a keel hauling. Those workouts become maintenance. I'm not saying that running before a swim workout is a bad thing. If that is the only time you have, then that is the way it has to be. But to improve your swimming, it is better to start the workout fresh. Just cut that day of running from the schedule.

During a swim phase, you want think of yourself not as a triathlete, or multisport athlete, but as a swimmer. Because the swim takes the least amount of time in the race, triathletes often tend to view it as a staging area for the bike leg. That may be the case, but if your swimming fitness is off, you will start your bike leg more fatigued. If you are working harder than you should, you will be depleting the glycogen stores not only in your arms but also in your legs. You will deplete your fuel sooner on the bike, which may take extra time and will definitely slow down your run. It's odd: During training it's best to take the sports individually, but during the race it all works together. It is important to exit the water feeling strong.

Time-efficient training is all about muscle recruitment. You want to recruit the most fibers in the least amount of time and learn to sustain high recruitment efforts. Your freestyle will benefit from practicing the other strokes, which will improve range of motion, strength, and muscle balance. Butterfly is a tremendous builder of strength and range of motion, not to mention character.

*M*any *triathletes resist doing nonfreestyle strokes like butterfly, backstroke, or breaststroke. When you practice all the strokes, you recruit more muscle fibers than if you practice only one.*

During a swim phase, you can spend three to five days in the water each week. Along with working on other strokes, you also want to spend time working on drills to improve your freestyle form (see chapter 7). No matter what your fitness level, an inefficient stroke can greatly reduce your speed. For at least two of the workouts, extend your time about a half hour over your previous workouts. Even more important than simply swimming more is adding to your main set. Try to get to a point where you do one of at least 2,000 yards or 25 minutes. More competitive athletes will want to swim five days per week, up to 3,000-yard main sets. Most people will improve on three days as long as they increase the main set over what they had been doing before.

*I*n *a time crunch, just one big main set can take a very short time. It can be better training than the same amount of swimming broken into smaller sets.*

While in a swim phase, you can keep your cycling to a couple of half-hour workouts on the stationary bike and two days of running per week. If short on time, you can also limit cycling or running to one workout in alternate weeks. That would mean one week you do two bike workouts and one run, and just opposite during the following week. Your swim workouts would build for three weeks, with an easy week during the fourth (see chapter 6).

Strong swimmers who swam competitively as kids tend to increase their swim performance faster. Those people may want to do a one-month tune-up in late winter. Others may want to do a couple of cycles in either fall or midwinter.

Once you have improved to a new level, holding it will be easy. A swim phase will involve three to five hours of swimming and one to three hours of combined running and cycling for a total training week of around six hours.

Be a Runner

Fall is really the best time for this concentration. Nothing will improve your fitness like racing, and fall 10Ks are abundant just about everywhere. You'll be amazed how fast you can run when you're not continually fatigued from cycling. You will always reach for a higher rung on the performance ladder during a race.

After your last triathlon, take a couple of weeks to a month or two without training. Stay active, but don't worry about a training schedule. Then return to your running schedule with a day of short intervals, a day of long intervals, and a long run

© Ken Lee

Finish each segment ready for the next one.

(see chapter 6). You will generally do better by increasing the number of repeats before increasing your pace, as long as your interval pace is as fast as your race pace. Your total running time can be as little as three hours, with a total training week of five hours. Running races without cycling will help to increase your maintained running speed.

During your running phase you can think of your cycling workouts as augmenting your running. You want to keep cycling sessions short but fairly intense. Unless you are building for a marathon, you can still improve by running three days per week. Occasional fourth days can help, but don't use running as recovery. If you feel that you need a recovery workout the day after a hard run, do an easy short bike ride. "Recovery run" is an oxymoron in the purist sense.

In chapter 7 we'll talk more about running form, but for now it's enough to know that the landing phase in a running stride can cause problems. If you do recovery workouts on the bike, you get blood flow to the areas needing repair without putting more landing stress on those fibers. Threshold time is also an important element in fitness improvement, and you can add to that with bike intervals, which will help your running.

Swimming can also help in recovery by alleviating any back stress brought on by running and softening that general "compressed" feeling from multiple landings.

Some people can do hard runs every other day, but for most people two days between hard runs works better. Don't do hard runs on consecutive days.

On the weeks when you don't have a race, hill runs are good. You can do them all year-round, but you want to cut back on hills and do more pacing work when you are actively racing. Chapter 6 will give some suggestions.

Be a Cyclist

If you've been doing some form of maintenance intervals on a stationary bike, increase your cycling time when the weather permits. Add some longer rides, with hills on odd weeks. The stationary bike will work for intervals two days per week, but it's more fun to get out on the road.

I haven't mentioned weight training yet, because it is not as important for swimming or running. Weights are more important for cycling because of the added force needed in the pedal stroke. It's getting back again to the old muscle recruitment issue. When you lift weights, you recruit just about every muscle fiber used in that particular movement. We don't want them to go to sleep. Two days of weight training with one additional ride of an hour or so will round out the week to four days of riding with two days of weights. The fourth day makes a big difference coming up from two or three maintenance days. A fifth will help during a cycling phase, but the returns begin to diminish with the increased time.

By building an intensity base you change the dynamics of lactic acid production and clearing. That metabolic process improves endurance performance. What makes up your $\dot{V}O_2$max is also metabolic. In a metabolic process, energy is produced through the burning of a fuel source. This all occurs inside the muscle cells. Cycling power comes from the nerves that fire the muscles. Think of it as training your wiring.

The power you can generate in a two-minute power test relates more closely to time trial performance than to $\dot{V}O_2$max. We'll go into greater depth in cycling power in chapter 8. Power is best measured by short-term efforts. So to build power, you want to practice sprinting. But all bike riding will have an impact on your power. Because cycling power is a neural function, simply repeating the movement helps. It's like a pianist practicing scales. During an easy ride of two hours, each foot will complete over 10,000 revolutions. In each pedal stroke, you learn how to do it more efficiently. Your neural system learns precisely when to fire specific muscle fibers to get the most power with the least effort.

To best improve muscle force and firing order, you need to work the muscle at least as hard and as fast as you would in a race. You should spend part of your training time simulating race conditions, going faster with short, intense intervals. Your race pace then becomes controlled. High-intensity sprints of 20 to 30 seconds with a rest of a minute to a minute and a half will do a great job of building power. Power workouts are short. On the stationary bike, they take 30 to 40 minutes. During a bike phase, you should spend one day per week with some type of sprint workout.

You might use another day of the week for two-minute threshold intervals. If you did a short time trial on another day and a longer easy ride on the weekend, you would have four days of cycling. You can do two and even three of the workouts indoors for extra time savings. During a bike building phase, you don't need to run more than two days, and both can be short. If you have already built your swimming, two days there will keep you where you left off. In alternate weeks you can either swim or run just once and probably not have a serious fitness loss.

A bike-building phase will involve more time per week than a building phase for the swim or run. While this is best done in the spring, you should consider other commitments to determine when you can accommodate the increased training time. This period will involve from five to eight hours per week, with three to four hours of cycling and an hour of weight training.

BALANCED TRAINING

OK, now you can begin to think of yourself as a duathlete or triathlete. It is best to have at least a month of balanced training before you have your first race. A good balanced plan will have three days per week in each sport. It will include a day of shorter intervals (about a minute), a day of longer intervals (2 to 10 minutes) or a time trial, and a longer easy effort. A total training time for international distance races will be in the eight- to nine-hour range. If you don't have that much time, it is better to eliminate a workout than to waste time with a haphazard one. For example, it is best to keep three days of cycling and eliminate a day of your stronger sport, either running or swimming. If it is a toss-up, then alternate weeks. With a schedule of two days per week in running and swimming, you can get the total week down to about six hours. It would total out to about three hours cycling, with running and swimming having an hour and a half each.

CROSS TRAINING

Now here is an argument that has run full circle. Back in the fabulous '80s, part of the appeal of triathlon was the cross-training aspect. Cross training is a principle that practicing one sport will help another. As more was learned about muscle specificity between disciplines, people began to realize that swimming 25,000 yards a week wasn't doing a thing for their running. Then specific training was in. For the most part, it still is. But more has been learned about cross training.

Cardiovascular Response

A large part of your fitness picture relies on the ability of your cardiovascular system to deliver oxygenated blood to your muscles. When you first begin training, your heart becomes stronger and pumps more blood with each beat. This is an

Let your kids get into the act. Your races can be as much fun for them as you.

increase in stroke volume. As I mentioned in chapter 1, this training response stays with you. Once you have been training on a regular basis for a year or more, any further cardiovascular changes will be minimal. On the other hand, if you have been fairly inactive and begin training, a cardiovascular change brought on by swimming helps with running and cycling and anything else that you do. An increase in the density of the capillaries surrounding the muscles that you have been training is a secondary response. The third response takes place within the muscle cells themselves. This last response is highly specific.

So a general rule is that the further along you are in your training, the more specific your training needs to be.

You can train both your cycling and running with bike workouts. The recovery is quicker from cycling because it doesn't involve the landing force of running.

Muscle Recruitment

New research consistently shows a specific cross-training response from cycling to running. Oddly, it doesn't work the other way. Of course, no one knows exactly why it is so, but I'll venture a guess. The muscle contraction of a pedal stroke is much more forceful than the contraction in a running stride. The stronger the contraction, the more fibers you recruit. When you are riding hard, you are recruiting not only specific cycling fibers but running ones as well. Thus, for cycling to have an effective cross-training effect, you need to have some intensity to increase fiber recruitment. By knowing this you can make your training time more efficient. Competitive runners have shown significant improvement by adding interval bike workouts to their programs. A multisport athlete gets a double benefit because the cycling workouts naturally help their bike riding. So even in a running phase, you will want to keep some cycling interval workouts as part of your program.

WEIGHT TRAINING: ESSENTIALS FOR SPECIFICITY

Weight training is a form of resistance exercise. The idea is to exercise with more resistance than you normally use in your sport. Stretch cords or your own weight can provide this in some instances. Although almost all resistance exercises are good for you, most will only give you balance in swimming, cycling, and running. If you want to keep your training time to a minimum, then you want to do specific exercises to recruit the muscle fibers used in your sports. You want your weight training to mimic closely the action that you are trying to strengthen.

As I mentioned previously, even though running and cycling recruit some of the same fibers, cycling involves a more forceful contraction. So weights will help cycling more than running. If your swimming stroke becomes shorter as you fatigue (almost everyone does this), weight training will help you to swim faster and maintain your speed longer.

A common problem in endurance sports is overuse injuries. Multiple contractions can break down and injure muscles, tendons, and ligaments. Resistance training can help strengthen these sport-specific body parts and help prevent these injuries. If you are training in more than one discipline, then you are already creating muscle balance, which also can help prevent injuries.

The goal of all training is to create a more powerful movement. Three factors—force, distance, and time—create power. The distance and time parts are best improved by performing your sport. Force is more easily enhanced through resistance training. Power = force × distance ÷ time. Force plays a role with distance in each pedal stroke in cycling (gear selection), in the pushoff in running (stride length), and in each stroke in swimming (distance covered). By creating more force, you strengthen the muscles that you need for a particular movement.

By using weights or another form of resistance, you can build muscle size. But as endurance athletes, we want only strength. Strength training is not body building. In most cases, you don't want to build muscle mass. In fact, bulky muscles will slow down an endurance athlete. A part of strength training is the recruitment of additional muscle fibers over those normally used. So in part, it is nerve training. Strength training as well as sprint work helps keep those motor units firing and alive. You build strength best by using enough weight or resistance to be difficult but not working the muscles to failure. That means if you complete 12 repetitions of a given weight, you could do 14 under a death threat. If you can complete 14 repetitions comfortably, you need more weight. Working in the range of 8 to 12 repetitions has been shown to be the most effective. You can do these exercises two or three days per week on non-consecutive days.

You should occasionally vary your workout. Sometimes do 20 reps with lighter weight. As a rule, it is best to work from larger muscle groups to smaller ones. This too can be reversed on occasional workouts to relieve weight room boredom.

The exercises outlined here are the basics. They will get you in and out of the weight room before you change age groups. Unless you change age groups in 20 minutes.

THE EXERCISES

Cycling—Muscles to train: quads, glutes, hamstrings, solei

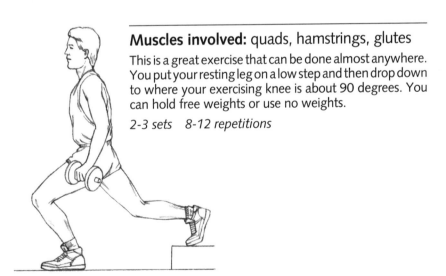

Muscles involved: quads, hamstrings, glutes

This is a great exercise that can be done almost anywhere. You put your resting leg on a low step and then drop down to where your exercising knee is about 90 degrees. You can hold free weights or use no weights.

2-3 sets   8-12 repetitions

One-leg squats

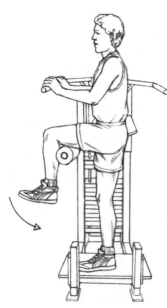

Hip extension

Muscles involved: glutes, hamstrings

Use the multihip machine for this exercise. Start with upper leg closer to your chest than a normal cycling angle. Pull leg down to where your knees are parallel to each other. This activates glutes more than the leg press does.

2-3 sets   8-12 repetitions

Seated calf raise

Muscles involved: solei

Recent studies show that this deep calf muscle is more involved in the power phase of a pedal stroke than previously thought. Use a seated calf machine or rest a barbell across the top of your knees (with a towel or pad). Raise up on your toes as far as you can. This is also good for running.

2-3 sets   8-12 repetitions

Back extension

Muscles involved: back extensors

These muscles exert a very force- ful stabilizing action every time your foot pushes down on the pedal. Your back will often weaken before your legs fatigue, diminish- ing the force you can apply to the pedals. Extend your head up from near the floor to no more than horizontal. Some people use weights on their shoulders. I don't think that's a good idea. This one shouldn't be as stressful as some of the others.

2-3 sets   10-15 repetitions

Caution: Effort should be comfortable on these. If you have back problems, this may not work for you. Don't do this one if it hurts at all. Try the back extension machine.

Running—Muscles to train: quads, hamstrings, solei, upper glutes

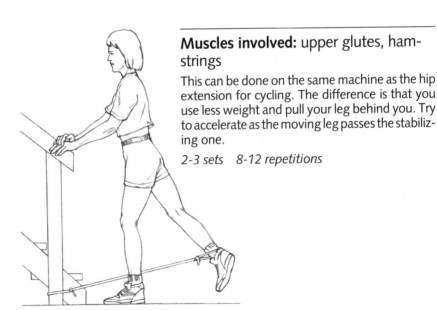

Hip hyperextension

Muscles involved: upper glutes, ham- strings

This can be done on the same machine as the hip extension for cycling. The difference is that you use less weight and pull your leg behind you. Try to accelerate as the moving leg passes the stabiliz- ing one.

2-3 sets   8-12 repetitions

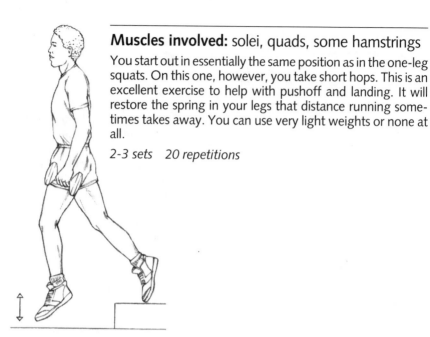

Muscles involved: solei, quads, some hamstrings

You start out in essentially the same position as in the one-leg squats. On this one, however, you take short hops. This is an excellent exercise to help with pushoff and landing. It will restore the spring in your legs that distance running sometimes takes away. You can use very light weights or none at all.

2-3 sets   20 repetitions

One-leg hops

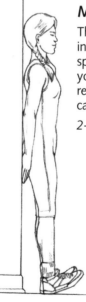

Muscles involved: tibialis anterior

This strengthens the muscles that first take the impact of landing. This is not a performance exercise, but it prevents shin splints. Lean back against a wall for stability and then raise up on your heels. Go up and down quickly without letting your feet rest on the ground. You can do this exercise without weight. It can also be done on a leg press machine.

2-3 sets   20 repetitions

Heel raises

Swimming—Muscles to train: lats, pecs, triceps, biceps, deltoids, and others

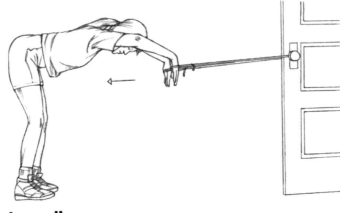

Swim pulls

Muscles involved: lats, pecs, triceps, deltoids, and a few more (swimming is a complex movement)

This is the closest you can get to swimming without getting wet. You can do this on a cable machine or with stretch cords. Keep your upper body in line with the cable or cord and pull in a swimming motion. The key is to keep your elbow high as you pull back. This will improve your distance per stroke.

2-3 sets   10-12 repetitions

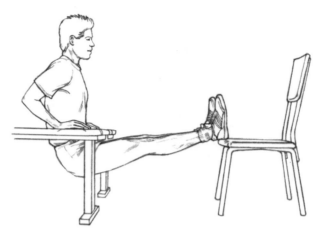

Dips

Muscles involved: triceps, deltoids, pecs

These help develop a strong finish to your swim stroke. They can be done on the Gravitron, or between two chairs or benches with your feet on a third chair. Dip down to where your elbow is bent past 90 degrees; then push back up.

Gravitron   2-3 sets   8-12 repetitions

Chair dips   2-3 sets   12-20 repetitions

TIME MANAGEMENT: THE WEEKLY SCHEDULE

© CLEO Photography

So far, we've been dealing with the generalities and ideas of saving training time. Now we're going to be specific about what goes into a week. How you set up your training week should fit in with your larger plan. Always keep in mind the direction that you want to go. Sometimes your training may not look as if it is part of the plan, but one instrument in an orchestra doesn't sound at all like a complete symphony.

---

*S*et up your training week beforehand.

Sometimes you should train strength and other times weakness. Throughout your training you want to take advantage of the principles of overload and maintenance. Everyone is a little different in this regard. It becomes a matter of priorities. If you want to go faster, and you haven't improved in a while, you will have to create more overload. It might only be the threshold time that you need to increase, which doesn't add much to the whole schedule, although it may feel like it. You also may have to increase total time. Everyone has different training responses, so you should monitor your progress or lack of it. The tests in chapter 2 will help keep you honest.

SETTING ASIDE THE TIME

When setting up your training the first question to answer is "How much time do I have this week?" No matter what your overall plan may be, you still have to take your training a week at a time. You know in advance what you plan to do each day. When plans change, you shuffle your workouts around. When you shuffle, you can put bike or swim workouts on consecutive days, but you should leave a day or two between runs.

Be realistic about the time commitment. It can get very discouraging to get into a week and realize on Friday that you still need 12 hours to complete your schedule.

*I*ntegrate training into your time schedule. Know when you will do your workouts. Put them in an appointment book if necessary.

The first step is considering other commitments and when you will do them. Then figure your total training time available. How you distribute your time among sports depends on whether you are in a building phase in one of them. A schedule that builds cycling takes more time than one that builds swimming or running. "What is the optimal amount of time in a balanced schedule?" you might ask. People new to multisport training will see improvements in six-hour weeks. People with experience can be highly competitive for international distance races with nine hours. Some people prefer to train in the morning before work. Others see morning workouts as a labor camp. It's better to plan your training for the time of day when you feel the best. Most people train best in the afternoon. If you have two workouts per day, you might do the one that you are trying to improve during your best time of the day.

Total Time and Time at Threshold

Sometimes a week with little total time but a high percentage of time at threshold can be more difficult than a longer week. So when you are building, you need to pay attention to how you are feeling after the workouts. Changing the emphasis of your schedule will help with freshness. Some weeks you will want to increase your time at or near threshold, and some weeks you should reduce it. Some weeks you might want to change your sport emphasis. The time at threshold will vary among the three sports but will always be greater during a build phase than when you are in a balanced schedule. In chapter 2 I gave a rough idea of time percentages at threshold—from 5 to 30 percent in running and cycling, and from 20 to 50 percent in swimming. Those are big ranges. You have to work up to increased time at threshold just as you gradually increase overall training time.

Anything that is above L2.5, or a perception of 14 on the Effort and Lactate Scale, can be considered threshold work. You almost never need to go over L4, or 16 (very hard). You should not go out and think that interval sessions should put you on the edge of death or wishing that you might die. You shouldn't dread your interval sessions. You don't need to push that hard. In fact, if you do, it can work against you. All you need to do is raise your blood lactate levels to the point of stimulating uptake. You know that you are working, but you are still comfortable. Don't make the mistake of confusing threshold work with burning speed sessions. Do anything above threshold, like bike sprints, for very short periods. And they're over before you know it.

A WEEK

As I outlined in the last chapter, you should make use of both balanced weeks and phase weeks. In the next chapter, I'll give some specific workouts and options. Below are some rough descriptions of a hypothetical balanced week. They give a general idea about how to split up your time.

You have seven hours in your total budget. The week outlined below is shown in chapter 6 as balanced week 1. Remember that when you look at your workout time, you count only time moving. Changing clothes doesn't count. Threshold time is anything above an L2 level.

In a running interval session of 200-meter repeats, your time at threshold is the time that it takes you to run each 200 multiplied by how many you do. The remainder of the time is usually easy running at an L1 level or slightly less. An example would be an athlete who runs a 10K in 44 minutes. That is a 7:06 pace, which makes a 200-meter repeat pace between 6:30 and 6:40. That works out to 50 seconds per 200.

If you did 10 of these 200s, your time at threshold would be just over 8 minutes (10 × 50 = 500 seconds ÷ 60 = 8+ minutes). If it takes roughly a minute and a half to jog a 200, which is a good rest for these intervals, you will have about 15 minutes of L1 running between repeats. With a 10-minute warm-up and 10-minute cool-down, your total time for the

workout is 43 minutes. Threshold running time of 8 minutes
calculates to 19 percent of your total time at threshold. If you
do a second run of 45 minutes at an L2 level, and a longer run
of 60 minutes, your total running time for the week is 2 hours
and 28 minutes. Use your total running time to calculate
threshold percentage, in this case 5 percent. If you haven't
been doing interval work, but have been consistently running
20 miles per week, this is a good week to start.

TOTAL THE TIME:

Workout #1—200s

Warm-up and cool-down total	=	20 min L1
Easy running between 200s	=	15 min L1
8 min of running 200s	=	8+ min L4
Total		43 min
L4 time = 8+ min	=	19% of 43 min

Workout #2—45 min L2   L4 time = 0

Workout #3—60 min L1   L4 time = 0

Total time 2 hr 28 min (43 min + 45 min + 60 min)
L4 time = 8 min = 5% of 148 min

Performance Progress Plus tracks all of this for you.

Let's stay within the bounds of about two and a half hours
of running because that is all the time you have. To get
stronger, you need to increase the difficulty of the workout to
recruit more muscle fibers. Even if you add no more time but
gradually increase the tempo of those 200-meter repeats, you
will be getting stronger. You should also add to the number of
repeats. If you took it up to 15 repeats, you would add about
12 minutes to the workout. Those 12 minutes are the overload
to your system. Those few extra minutes are what will change
your fitness and performance. At this point, you would have
2 hours 39 minutes total running time, with 12 minutes at

threshold, bringing your percentage up to about 7 percent. You will hardly notice the difference in time. You can do the same thing with cycling and swimming.

TOTAL THE TIME:

Workout #1—200s

Warm-up and cool-down total	=	20 min L1
Easy running between 200s	=	22 min L1
15 × 200 at 50 s	=	12+ min L4
Total		54 min
L4 time 12+ min	=	23% of 54 min

Workout #2—45 min L2 L4 time = 0

Workout #3—60 min L1 L4 time = 0

Total time 2 hr 39 min (54 min + 45 min + 60 min)
L4 time = 12 min = 7% of 159 min

We still have four and a half hours to juggle. In a balanced phase of training, it's best to devote two 45-minute workouts to swimming and a total of three hours to cycling. One of the best training time savers is the stationary bike or a windtrainer. It's amazing what you can accomplish in a half hour.

On the stationary bike, you could do one workout to build power and another to raise your threshold. Sprints of 20 to 30 seconds will build your power. These should be about 25 percent higher than your threshold level. So if your threshold is at 200 watts, or roughly 21 miles per hour, your sprint should be at 250 watts, or 24 miles per hour (200 × 125 percent = 250). If you did 10 of these for 20 seconds, you could figure 3 minutes into your threshold time (20 × 10 = 200 seconds ÷ 60 = 3+ minutes). This can be a little misleading as to effort, because those are very big minutes. This supra-maximal effort (above aerobic capacity) is possible for very brief periods. It's amazing how long a time 20 seconds can be when you are at an effort above your aerobic capacity. So it's a wise policy to give yourself the option to call the workout good at five sprints. Your threshold work would be at 200 watts, or 21 miles an hour, for repeats of 1 to 5 minutes with a shorter or equal amount of rest. You can complete each of these workouts in 30 minutes. A two-hour ride at L1 (fairly light) keeps your cycling week at three hours. Adding just a few repeats to either the threshold workout or the sprint session will cause an overload with a time increase of just a few minutes. If you did 10 sprints on one day, and 10 one-minute threshold repeats on another day, your total threshold time works out to 13 minutes, or 7 percent. By increasing your sprints to 15 and adding 5 repeats of 1 minute each, you have increased your total time to 3 hours and 23 minutes with a threshold time of 20 minutes, or roughly 10 percent.

Ride or run to work. This isn't for everyone, but if you can combine your commute and training, you are a master of saving time.

Shorten recovery time in threshold work. Simply reducing the amount of rest during a workout brings improvement. The time saving is obvious.

To complete the week, we have an hour and a half of swimming. It doesn't sound like much, but it can work. Many people will even improve with this; for others it will be maintenance.

In this balanced week example, I've left the least amount of time for swimming because you will spend less time there in a race. If swimming is your weak area, then you may want to give it slightly more emphasis on odd weeks. You definitely want to devote a part of your year to a swim phase. For now, we'll work with just two workouts. For two swim sessions to do the most good, one should build speed and power, and the other should build threshold and endurance. (Many people can swim fast, but the water quickly turns to glue.) Repeats of 50s and 25-yard (or meter) sprints build speed and power, 150s and 200s build threshold and endurance, and 300s and above build endurance. Your repeatable effort for 200s with a rest of about 30 seconds is close to what you should be able to hold in a mile race. A workout with 50s as the repeat distance with 10 to 15 seconds of rest builds the speed that you can hold for the 200s. Faster 50s with a minute of rest are power builders.

In a 45-minute workout, you could do a set of 15 × 50 at an L2.5 level with 10 to 20 seconds of rest. Then do a set of 10 × 50, swimming the first 25 as a sprint and swimming the second 25 at an easy pace. The rest could be easy swimming or kicking. For average swimmers, this will come out to 18 minutes at threshold. On another day a set of 7 × 150 and a set with some stroke work would have a threshold time of around 20 minutes. Your total threshold time for the week is 38 minutes, which is 42 percent. You could make this week a little harder by adding two 150s and another five 50s. With 8 to 12 minutes of additional swimming, the threshold increases to 46 percent.

Remember that although your workouts may look more difficult on paper as you progress, your training adaptions will keep the effort unchanged.

The total week in its beginning state is just under seven hours. The total of increases for all three sports is 48 minutes. Once you have adapted to a week like the sample, the extra 48 minutes will continue the progress by providing an overload. In most cases people will add to only one or two of the sports, so you can figure on an increase of 20 or 30 minutes over a week, bringing your total up to seven and a half hours.

You will see in the next chapter that the threshold percentages may look high during a maintenance week in a sport. The actual time training may be short, but because a maintenance week in a sport often has only two workouts, a small amount of threshold time constitutes a large percentage. The percentages explained above assume a week with some distance work at an easy level.

IS IT IMPROVEMENT OR MAINTENANCE?

Your training will do one of three things. You will improve, you will stay the same, or you will decline. Once your body adjusts to training load, you will have to do more to improve. As we've seen previously, it doesn't take much extra time. Overload must be only a little bit more. If you do less than your adapted training load, at first you will likely hold your fitness level. Your body resists change at first, so maintenance is easy. If your training load is less than half the time you spent gaining fitness, and your intensity is less, then you will slowly lose fitness. If you overload too much—add too much time or intensity too fast—you will overtrain. You will lose fitness. Undertraining is better. You get the same effect with a lot less work.

If you've done one or more triathlons in the last year, the best way to identify your weak sport is to look at the race results and your relative placing in each segment.

STRENGTH AND WEAKNESS BETWEEN SPORTS

Even in a balanced phase of training, you will still want to pay attention to a weakness. You have strength and weakness both between sports and within sports. Of course it always comes back to the original time budget. You will benefit the most from working a weakness. Improvements are smaller and take more time when working on a strength.

Isolating the weak sport is usually easier than isolating a specific weakness within it. Most people know where they fall behind. People passing you is a fairly good sign. Your relative performance on the segments may vary from race to race, but you will usually see a pattern. There is no argument that the most time can be made up or lost on the bike. But if you are swimming 10 minutes slower than your nearest competitor and riding 5 minutes faster, your efforts should go to the swim. You can overcome the 5-minute deficit more quickly in the water.

I've found that people who have been doing one of the triathlon sports for a number of years and have only recently begun the other two are not always stronger in their mainstay area. It could be that you have been running for the last 15 years and for some reason have a large amount of cycling power. Your aerobic capacity may be higher as a runner, but your performance potential could be greater as a cyclist. So now what do you do? In the last chapter we mentioned that cycling has a cross-training effect to running but that the opposite effect doesn't exist. The emphasis in training should go to the bike. This kind of person would benefit most from threshold-raising and threshold-drift workouts. Highly competitive runners, on the other hand, are often short on cycling power, and need a cycling emphasis with attention to sprints and short hills.

Some commutes are longer than others.

Another common scenario is the swimmer who began at age five and competed in college. Even after long layoffs, it's astounding how fast these people can regain swimming fitness. In a single three-week build period, most are ready for a two-day-a-week maintenance program for the rest of the season. This athlete should look to cycling or running for a concentration.

I've heard it said that triathlon began as a swimmers' sport. I don't know where the notion began, but don't believe it for a minute. Triathlon favors strong cyclists. A competitive cyclist has a strong edge over any other single-sport specialist. Assuming a large difference in abilities, swimmers can't get far enough ahead, and fast runners can't catch up. The problem for racing cyclists is usually swimming. Their sport, and running, can leave a wasteland of an upper body. Cyclists can often run well but need a long period of swim emphasis. Too often, strong cyclists are unable to take advantage of their abilities because the swim took too long and made them too tired. Everyone should exit the water with a minimum amount of fatigue. Without this fatigue, the cyclist who is a reasonably fit swimmer can often fake a 10K run. Two days a week in the pool is enough.

You might be a stronger cyclist than swimmer. But in cycling, while you can hammer on the flats and short hills, you fall behind in long hills. If you never race on a course with long hills, it doesn't matter much. But if you have a hilly event coming up, then your time is best spent riding long hills and swimming.

There are endless individual scenarios. And how you split up your time depends on your goals. In a race, the three sports generally play out like this: The swim is a staging area. If you are a slow swimmer, you miss the start of the bicycle race. The bike segment is where you can make up or lose the most time. The last half of the run determines placing. Whoever wants it the most gets in front.

WEAKNESSES WITHIN SPORTS

No one has it all. Most of us are good at many things and poor at many others. You can have a low threshold, but a lot of power and speed. You can have just the opposite. You can have a high threshold, but not be able to sustain it for long, which means that you have a lactate and $\dot{V}O_2$ drift. You can have a high or low $\dot{V}O_2$max. And you can have all sorts of combinations of the above between the different sports. Have I lost you yet? Wait, this isn't as complicated as it sounds.

The best way to know your strengths and weaknesses with any accuracy is to be tested. There are also some fairly strong indicators that you can determine through your workouts. You may already have an idea. Let's take a look at what you can do about some problems.

Threshold

Without doing a maximal test, it's hard to know at what percentage of max your threshold lies. Your heart rate at threshold should be in the range of 85 to 95 percent of maximum heart rate. Higher is better. If it is under 80 percent then you can consider it low.

Remember that 15 to 16 on the Effort and Lactate Scale is considered threshold. In chapter 3 I described a test to give your maximum heart rate. It tends to be about 3 to 5 beats lower for cycling and 10 beats lower for swimming. Even if you don't know your exact percentage, you can track changes by pace and heart rate. Beginning athletes may find that a threshold effort is very near an all-out effort. This can look like a high threshold relative to max. From a numbers standpoint this is true, but it doesn't convert to performing at or near that level. This is mostly due to an inhibition to go to a true all-out effort. More fit athletes with competition experience usually don't have this inhibition.

Threshold Drift

If you can go fast for very short distances but have trouble sustaining a harder effort, then you have drift. A drift problem also rears its ugly head during a workout when your repeat times become progressively slower. If your last two miles in a 10K are 30 or more seconds per mile slower than your first two, you have a drift situation. You can have a very high threshold and considerable drift. This is a common problem with beginning people and those who have not changed their training in a while. They have a certain tolerance that remains static. No matter what distance or sport, your paces should remain relatively constant. We tend to look at an overall time and average it for a pace rather than looking at distance splits. The difference between running a 5K and 10K is a prime example. Most people don't start a 10K much slower; they just fade to a slower pace. That brings down the average. Usually the perceived effort is much higher at the end, but the pace is slower.

Pacing or tempo efforts help with this problem. Sustained efforts at just under a threshold level for 20 minutes are a big help in all three sports. You can also do workouts at that pace or efforts with 3- to 5-minute repeats with very short rest.

Speed and Power

In cycling, the biggest thing keeping you from going faster is wind drag, which increases exponentially with speed. Air and water behave similarly, so drag in the water is the same problem. Muscle force and speed are necessary to overcome that drag. If you can use a smaller percentage of your short-term maximal power in longer sustained efforts, you will be able to hold a faster pace. Think of it as a power reserve. If you can sprint on a bike at 35 miles per hour, holding 25 miles per hour is a much different task than it would be if you could sprint only 27 miles per hour. This would still be the case if you had a high threshold and a small amount of drift. If you ride with a group and sprint up a short hill, the most powerful riders are the ones who surge ahead.

This is where 20- and 30-second sprints with full recovery come into play. Efforts above threshold for two minutes or less also help. They are harder to do. This is one time that you need to break the rule of threshold work being comfortably hard. This is speed work and is anything but comfortable. Two-minute efforts above threshold are downright painful. A 20-second sprint will begin to make a change, and the time is up before it gets too uncomfortable. You only want go through training phases of this stuff for a couple of months at most. Mentally, it can fry you. The good part is that changes come quickly, so you don't need to do it for very long.

Aerobic Capacity

On the bike and run, people with high aerobic capacity ($\dot{V}O_2$max) tend to climb long hills well. You can almost take a group and have them race up a 10-minute hill and tell their relative aerobic capacity by the order of placing. As I said in chapter 1, part of your aerobic capacity is determined at conception, and there is nothing you can do about it. Fat cigar smokers who are very talented can outrace highly trained people on ideal diets. It just doesn't happen very often, because the fat smokers have chosen a lifestyle that doesn't include much activity. Your $\dot{V}O_2$max will undergo the most change during the first year or two of your training. It may change slightly after that, but most of your performance will come from other avenues.

Studies have shown that both low-intensity distance work and higher intensity interval work will improve your $\dot{V}O_2$max. All training will tend to improve it during your first couple of years of regular training. You can still raise it after that, but you may not like the effort necessary. Remember that people with high capacity tend to excel in long all-out climbs. To give your $\dot{V}O_2$max that final tweak, you need to do just that—long climbs at a maximal effort. It's an option. Two or three times a month in your weak sport, for three months, will raise it.

I wouldn't continue this kind of work on a year-round basis. I've had some very fit people who need a little $\dot{V}O_2$max boost complain long and loud about these workouts.

ROTATE EMPHASIS

No matter what your strength or weakness, everyone can benefit from a rotation of emphasis. It helps keep you fresh and makes the best use of the overload and maintenance principles. You can only overload for a limited time before staleness sets in. Maintenance for too long can turn to a decline. This especially holds true during the triathlon off-season. If you have a single-sport preference, you can concentrate on other areas at times. The fall has cross-country races and many Halloween runs and turkey trots. Winter and early spring is short-course season for masters swimming, and many bicycle races are scheduled in spring.

Now with my argument established about training weakness, you also can consider the other side. For most of us it's more fun to train a strong sport, to use our natural talent. Training a weakness is usually going against the grain. Although the odds of improving a weakness are better, if you can make up the same amount of time training a strength, go for it.

6

TIMETABLES AND SAMPLE WORKOUTS

© Ken Lee

Most people have a simple request of a training book or a coach: "Just tell me what to do." This chapter provides that guidance. In the following workout suggestions, we'll take all the factors that we've been covering and put them into a training week. You don't have to do these workouts exactly as prescribed, but they give an idea about the type of workout to do. You can add to them or cut them back. None of them should give you the fear that the end of your life is at hand. They are supposed to be fun. You should finish with the feeling that you could have done more. I mean that.

You will need some definitions.

(40 s) — Any number in parentheses indicates rest. In some cases it is standing rest; in others it is active rest. Cycling rest is always active. Swimming rest is wall time.

(200 L1) — This would mean 220 yards or 200 meters of easy running recovery. You will find that as you recover, you might start running slightly faster. This indicates a quick recovery and is good. Just keep the effort the same. Your pace will be fairly slow for the first 30 seconds or so.

10-12 × 400 — You have an option. You can do 10 to 12 quarter-mile or 400-meter repeats. You could also do 4 or 5. If you reach a point where you feel you can't continue, then don't. You always want to leave the workout able to have done more.

L1, L2, L2.5, L4 — Lactate levels by perceived exertion. Do these workouts first by perceived effort; then check pace, and finally check heart rate. If you note that your heart rate and pace have gone up with no change in perceived effort, your threshold has risen. Congratulations!

Strks — This is an abbreviation for strokes in swim workouts. It means to swim nonfreestyle, in other words, butterfly, backstroke, or breaststroke. It's your choice.

IM — This is short for individual medley. You swim butterfly, then backstroke, then breaststroke, then freestyle. Non-butterflyers may substitute freestyle. If you have knee problems, do breaststroke without kicking, or do a dolphin kick, like in butterfly.

Kick/swim — This means to kick the first half of the repeat and swim the second half. So a 100 kick/swim means to kick 50 and then swim 50. Unless otherwise specified, this is all freestyle.

Lap — In swimming, a lap is one length of the pool. Everywhere else you go, you will find that a lap gets you back to where you started. A swimming lap leaves you at the other end of the pool.

Progressive — This means that you continually get faster on each repeat during the set.

• — This is the beginning of a set. You can take a break between sets. Don't go out for a sandwich and a beer; just take a minute or so.

If a range is given, the total time of a workout is figured on the larger number of repeats. If a set says 8-12 × 2 min hills L4, it means that you climb a hill for two minutes 8 to 12 times at an L4 level. The total amount is figured on 12 times, even though it is an option. The L4 time is the amount of time you spend at that level of exertion.

Any workout with a level of L2.5 or above is considered threshold work for time purposes. You are training your lactate clearing rates at that level, so you can take any workout that gives an L4 prescription and back off a bit. The training response is more profound as you go to higher intensity, but the higher intensity gets painful. You may not want to do that. No one can fault you for avoiding pain. Most will applaud your intelligence. A training response requires only that you do a little more than you have previously done. You are the best judge of how intense and long your workout should be. You may want to add repeats, shorten rest, or lengthen the rest and cut the number of repeats.

When a set is given in distance (e.g., 400 m), the time of the workout is an approximation. You may go slightly faster and have less total time or slower and have more. I use the time suitable for people in the middle of the field. You may have to adjust the times to fit your pace. In the running workouts with distance prescriptions (e.g., 200), you may substitute the time it should take you to complete the distance and do them on the road or trail.

I've given some consecutive running days in the run emphasis weeks. Occasionally, you can do this. In the bigger picture,
successive days of running take lots of time and add little or
no fitness. An occasional spike in your running time will help.

If the plan calls for two workouts on one day, it is usually
best to separate them. It is easier to swim first. As you
approach race season, you will want to do bike and run
workouts back-to-back (brick), but otherwise you should split
them. Run first when you are in a run phase. Mix it up when
you are in a bike phase.

The days off are mixed in the samples to give you an idea
about options in setting up a week. Most people use the same
day each week for their no-training day. It doesn't matter. You
can mix it, or it can stay the same. Make the training fit your
schedule.

These sample weeks vary in difficulty. The third one in each
group is the hardest. Total time and time at threshold are
indicators of difficulty, but some workouts are harder than
they appear. You will see that some of the workouts have time,
pace, or power prescriptions. Performance Progress Plus calculates these, based on individual fitness data. The ones given
are for examples only. Your paces or power ranges will
probably differ.

SWIM EMPHASIS

The following weeks are designed to build swimming while
keeping cycling and running to a maintenance level. Remember that maintenance requires you to maintain intensity for
only half of the time that it took you to improve. An important
element in sport rotation is that your maintenance workouts
don't leave you fatigued for your key workouts. Use them as a
break, a diversion.

It's usually best to swim first if a day has two workouts,
especially during a swim phase. If a day has a bike and a run
workout, do the emphasis sport first. You want to be fresh for
your improvement area. If you are tired, you will just practice
being tired and going slowly. Otherwise, it's generally better to
run first early in the season and bike first as you approach
races.

More people have trouble with swimming than with the other two sports, so I am going to give some examples for people who need form work before gaining fitness. No matter how fit your swimming muscles, your progress will come to a standstill with poor form. If you are working on form, you should take extra rest. Don't practice being tired and slow. If the distance is too great, shorten it. If you begin to lose form after 25 meters or yards, then just practice 25s. Do the Monday swim in week 1 on the other days as well. Take as much rest as you need to repeat your best form.

These weeks give an idea about some options; you need not do them in order. Because everyone is different, some of these workouts may be too hard or too easy. You may need to adjust the plan so that the following weeks will challenge your swimming while allowing maintenance with cycling and running.

Week 1 Swim Emphasis

Monday swim: If you are starting as a swimmer, I can't emphasize enough the repetition of proper form. Chapter 7 will give you some ideas. One- and two-lap repeats will give you practice without fatiguing you. The more you practice a bad habit, the more difficult it is to correct. The 25s on this workout are not hard, but you shouldn't swim them at a slow pace. Good form is practiced best at a moderate, or L2, pace. The kick swims are a good exercise to practice proper kick/stroke timing (see chapter 7). I have some people do only this kind of workout, nothing harder, until they have begun to create good form habits.

Tuesday swim: In the 150s you build your speed in the odd-numbered laps so that you finish at nearly a sprint pace. The even-numbered laps are active recovery. The 75s are nonfreestyle during the first lap.

Tuesday run: You just pick up your pace to an L4 or 5K race pace for about 20 seconds and then run at an L1 level until you have fully recovered. You just throw in these pickups when you feel like it.

Wednesday bike: If you use a heart rate monitor, don't look for a heart rate to get to an L4 level for at least five repeats. Remember that heart rate lags behind exercise. Because of threshold drift, the first few repeats probably won't feel quite like L4.

Thursday swim: I give a range of five to ten 50s, and for more experienced swimmers it can even be more. The first group of 50s are pacing work. This is a pace that you can't quite hold for longer distances. The sprint 25s are to build power and speed.

Saturday swim: The first set is a ladder in which you go up to 150 and then come back down to 50. You go through this cycle two or three times. You go directly from one cycle to the next unless you absolutely must have a bonus rest between them. Work up so that you can complete a few rotations without a break.

Saturday run: While written as a track workout, you don't have to do it there. You can run for time on the road or a trail. It's good to have known distances, but you can run for time. In the example, at a 7:00-mile pace, you would run for 3:30.

		Swim	Bike	Run
Week 1 — Swim Emphasis	**MON**	• 300 warm-up • 10-20 × 25 (15 s) work on perfect form • 5-10 × 50 kick/swim (20 s) `20` min total `0` min L4		
	TUES	• 300 warm-up • 3-5 × 150, odd laps build speed, even L1 (15 s) • 6 × 75 alt strokes 1st lap (10 s) • 150 cool-down `50` min total `15` min L4		• 10 min warm-up • 45 min L1 w/5 × 100 yd pickups, full L1 recovery between `55` min total `0` min L4
	WED		• Stationary • 5 min warm-up • 5-10 × 1 min L4 239 watts (1 min L1) • 5 min cool-down `30` min total `10` min L4	
	THURS	• 300 warm-up • 5-10 × 50 L2.5 (15 s) • 10 × 50 sprint 25, easy 25 (15 s) • 200 L2 • 150 cool-down `45` min total `25` min L4		
	FRI			
	SAT	• 300 warm-up • 2-3 × 50, 100, 150, 100, 50 L2; 2:03/100 (20 s) • 3 × 100 swim 50/kick 50 (15 s) • 100 cool-down `45` min total `0` min L4		• 10 min warm-up • 3-5 × 800 L2.5-L4 7:00 pace (45 s-1 min) Hr under 169 • 10 min cool-down `45` min total `17` min L4
	SUN		• 1 hr L1 `60` min total `0` min L4	
		Total 2:40 **L4** 0:40 24.9%	**Total** 1:30 **L4** 0:10 11.1%	**Total** 1:40 **L4** 0:17 17.0%
			Weekly total 5:50	

Week 2 Swim Emphasis

Tuesday swim: The first group of 50s resembles a broken 250 or 500. You swim at a pace faster than you normally would for that distance, and the short rest allows you to maintain it.

The second group of 50s builds speed, so you should do these a couple of seconds faster than the first group. The third group increases the pace yet again, but you only have to do it for a 25.

Wednesday run: You can do this run on the track, or on the road for the time it would take you to complete 200 meters or 220 yards, at a pace slightly faster than threshold. You will start the L1 running as a slow jog, but you should gradually increase speed as you recover. You should keep the same effort throughout the recovery period.

Thursday bike: This is a higher power output than you could maintain for a minute. Take more than the 1:40 rest if you need it. You want to consistently reach this high level for a brief period.

Friday run: This is a good one to do on an out-and-back course. It is best if you have some marked distances somewhere on your route to check your pace. These paces make good entries into Performance Progress Plus to check your fitness improvement.

If you don't have marked distances, during your 5-minute L1 go 2-1/2 minutes, and then turn around and start back from the point that ended your 12-minute L2. From this point, running at L2.5, you should reach your starting point before 12 minutes. If your effort rose, but your pace didn't, try this workout again in about three weeks. If your pace quickens after three weeks, you have changed your threshold drift (see chapter 1).

Sunday swim: If you find that your pace begins to slow on the set of 150s (don't worry, this happens to most people), take a break for about a minute and start again. Do this as often as you think is necessary to maintain your pace. Watch your time to see whether you need the extra rest. That in itself will transfer to better race performances.

On the set of 100s, make the last 100 free the fastest swimming of the entire workout.

		Swim	Bike	Run
Week 2 — Swim Emphasis	**MON**	• 300 warm-up • 10-20 × 25 (15 s) work on perfect form • 5-10 × 50 kick/swim (20 s) **20** min total **0** min L4		
	TUES	• 300 warm-up • 5-10 × 50 L2.5 (10 s) 56 s • 5-10 × 50 L4 (20 s) 54 s • 5-10 × 50 sprint 25, 25 L1 (15 s) **45** min total **22** min L4	• 10 min warm-up • 5 × 1:30 L4 (1:30 L1) • 5 min cool-down **30** min total **7** min L4	
	WED			• 10 min warm-up • 7 × 200 ~ 49 s (200 L1) keep running throughout workout • 10 min cool-down **36** min total **6** min L4
	THURS	• 300 warm-up • 3-5 × 300 L2 (30 s) 2:03/100 • 4 × 100 kick L2 (20 s) • 100 cool-down **55** min total **0** min L4	• Stationary • 5 min warm-up • 5-10 × 20 s sprint (1:40) 383 watts • 5 min cool-down **30** min total **3** min L4	
	FRI			• 10 min warm-up • 12 min L2 • 5 min L1 • 12 min L2.5 7:18 pace • 10 min cool-down **50** min total **12** min L4
	SAT			
	SUN	• 300 warm-up • 7 × 150 L2.5 (15 s) • 5 × 100 (30 s) odd #s free even #s strks (free 100s are progressive) • 150 cool-down **40** min total **21** min L4		• 1 hr L1 **60** min total **21** min L4
		Total 2:40 **L4** 0:43 26.8%	**Total** 1:00 **L4** 0:10 10.0%	**Total** 2:26 **L4** 0:39 26.7%
		Weekly total 6:06		

Week 3 Swim Emphasis

Monday swim: The first set is for form. Most people need to practice rolling to their nonbreathing side. The second set is for pacing. The 50s should be fairly comfortable as you learn the pace designed for the 200s. The 100s should be slightly more challenging, while the 200s should be difficult. Swim the 50s so that you swim the same pace the entire set.

Monday run: Use a grade of 6 to 8 percent. You want to feel as if you are running with added resistance, so your form is close to how you would run on a flat. Steeper hills give the sensation of climbing, not running. Add some rest time after you jog back to your starting point.

Tuesday swim: This should start out as an L1 effort but usually becomes L2 at the end. Try to hold the same pace.

Tuesday bike: You simply increase your effort and power output. There is no rest between increases. Over time, try to hold an L4 effort for five minutes at the end.

Wednesday swim: This reads easier than it is. The 300s are all fairly comfortable, and you should feel mostly recovered during the rest (take more rest if you need it). Do the 100s in the tightest time interval that you can maintain. If your L4 effort is 1:30, you would leave on a 1:40 send-off interval. The same holds true for the 50s and 25s. They should feel easier than the 100s. As you progress, change the workout to 400s and 4 × 100, 8 × 50, and 16 × 25.

Friday bike: Pick a grade on which you stay seated for most of the climb. This helps build the glutes, which are a primary power producer.

Friday run: Do this right around your 10K race pace. Go to effort level before thinking about heart rate or pace.

Saturday swim: The first set is 5 × 100. You just pick up the pace slightly during the second half. This is a fairly easy set. The 50s are five groups of three, with every third one being fast. Think of the first 50 in each group as a recovery from the fast one that preceded it.

The last group of 100s are very fast. Take more rest if you need it. (Almost time for a sandwich and a beer.)

Sunday swim: Both groups of 200s are on the same send-off interval. You get more rest on the second group because you are swimming them faster. You can shorten this if you like.

		Swim	Bike	Run
Week 3 — Swim Emphasis	**MON**	• 300 warm-up • 5 × 50 practice rolling (20 s) • 8 × 50, 4 × 100, 1 × 200 L2.5 (20 s) hold 1:57/100 • 4 × 100 kick/swim (15 s) **45** min total **12** min L4		• 10 min warm-up • 6-8 × 2 min moderate hills L4 (3:30 with jog down to start) • 10 min cool-down **50** min total **16** min L4
	TUES	• 300 warm-up • 2,000 L2 • 150 cool-down **45** min total **0** min L4	• Stationary • 5 min warm-up • 5 min L1, 5 min L2, 5 min L2.5, 2 min L4 239 watts • 5 min cool-down **30** min total **10** min L4	
	WED	• 300 warm-up • 300 L1 (30 s) 3 × 100 L4 (10 s) • 300 L1 (30 s) 6 × 50 L4 (10 s) • 300 L1 (30 s) 12 × 25 L4 (5 s) • 150 cool-down **50** min total **20** min L4		
	THURS			
	FRI		• 15 min warm-up • 7-12 × 2 min L4 seated climbs (2 min rest riding back to start) • 15 min cool-down **78** min total **24** min L4	• 10 min warm-up • 3-5 × 5 min L2.5-4 (5 min L1) Hr 164 7:18 pace • 10 min cool-down **70** min total **25** min L4
	SAT	• 300 warm-up • 5 × 100, 50 L1, 50 L2 (25 s) • 15 × 50, 5 × (#1 easy #2 build #3 fast) (15 s) • 5 × 100 L4+ (1:30) **50** min total **20** min L4		
	SUN	• 300 warm-up • 5 × 200 L2 (15 s) • 5 × 200 L2.5 (25 s) hold same interval as L2 200s • 5 × 100 kick 50/swim 50 (15 s) **45** min total **19** min L4		
		Total 3:55 **L4** 1:11 30.2%	**Total** 1:48 **L4** 0:34 31.4%	**Total** 2:00 **L4** 0:41 34.1%
		Weekly total 7:43		

BIKE EMPHASIS

An important consideration in a bike emphasis is that your running may also improve. Naturally good runners might want to spend most of their racing season in some form of bike emphasis. If a swim period preceded the bike period, you will do well with two days of swimming per week. If time allows, you can increase the workouts, but still swim two days. You might still be improving.

Week 1 Bike Emphasis

Monday swim: This is a maintenance workout. You can raise the intensity if you like.

Tuesday bike: This is a classic time-saving workout. Some people refer to it as "minute on, minute off." You gradually want to see an L4 power increase. As you become more fit, add a few repeats after you have increased your power.

Wednesday and Friday bike: Every time your foot goes around in a pedal cycle, learning occurs. Many people tend to ride too hard when they should go easy, which doesn't allow enough recovery to go hard when they should. Go easy when it says Ll.

Saturday bike: If you have some flat sections, check your pace against past and future workouts.

Sunday bike: This is essentially an easy ride with some intermittent hill pickups. Just increase your effort as you get to any hills.

	Swim	Bike	Run
MON	• 300 warm-up • 7 × 50 L2 (10 s) 56 s • 7 × 50 L4 (20 s) 54 s • 7 × 50 sprint 25, 25 L1 (15 s) `45` min total `22` min L4		
TUES		• Stationary • 5 min warm-up • 5-10 × 1 min L4 239 watts (1 min L1) • 5 min cool-down `30` min total `10` min L4	
WED		• 45-60 min L1 `60` min total `0` min L4	• 10 min warm-up • 7-200 ~ 49 s (200 L1) keep running throughout workout • 10 min cool-down `36` min total `6` min L4
THURS			
FRI		• 45-60 min L1 `60` min total `0` min L4	
SAT		• 15 min warm-up & cool-down • 7 × 2 min L2, 2 min L1 • 5 × 1 min L4, 1 min L1 L2 should be about 19 mph on flats `68` min total `5` min L4	• 10 min warm-up • 12 min L2 • 5 min L1 • 12 min L2 8:18 pace • 10 min cool-down `50` min total `12` min L4
SUN	• 300 warm-up • 3 × 300 L2 (30 s) 2:03/100 • 2 × 100 kick L2 (20 s) • 100 cool-down `40` min total `0` min L4	• 1 hr-1 hr 30 min L1 over rolling course, L2.5 uphill sections `90` min total `0` min L4	
	Total 1:25 **L4** 0:22 25.8%	**Total** 5:08 **L4** 0:15 4.9%	**Total** 1:26 **L4** 0:18 20.9%
		Weekly total 7:59	

Week 1 — Bike Emphasis

Week 2 Bike Emphasis

Tuesday swim: You just go up in intensity with 150-yard (or meter) repeats. Note that you get more rest at L4.

Tuesday bike: You will need a stationary bike that has variable resistance to do this workout. Your power output remains the same on each group of sprints (see "Cycling Power" in chapter 8). Some bikes will hold a constant power and adjust the resistance to your cadence. So with slower cadence you have more resistance, and with higher cadences you have less resistance. It is preferable to have a bike on which you can adjust the resistance yourself. The first group is at high cadence with a lower resistance. You move up the resistance and slow your cadence on the next two groups of four sprints. You can add or cut back the number of repeats to suit your level or motivation.

Wednesday run: This is similar in spirit to a swim workout in swim week 3. The first part is comfortable. You run at a pace that is easy for a quarter mile, but difficult for a mile. A word of warning: Don't go too fast on the 400s. Save yourself. During a run phase, do two miles at the end.

Friday run: All the running on a flat or uphill is easy. You simply go fast on the downhill sections for about 30 seconds. You can zigzag if you like. It's easier on your joints if you do this on dirt. This is a very effective workout, and it's beneficial all year. But even on dirt, it can be hard on knees, ankles, and back. If you have trouble in any of those areas, you may not want to do this one.

Saturday bike: Do this workout on a road similar to the one you used on the Sunday workout in week 2, but here you do standing short sprints for 10 to 30 seconds. Ride easy the rest of the time. Just sprint when you get to a hill. Let the road dictate how often you do it. As you become more fit, try a more challenging road.

Sunday bike: This is your longer easy ride. You can go longer if you like. Include some longer climbs if you have such a route.

Week 2 — Bike Emphasis

	Swim	Bike	Run
MON			
TUES	• 300 warm-up • 3 × 150 L2 (15 s), 3 × 150 L2.5 (30 s), 2 × 150 L4, (1:30), 3 × 150 L2.5 (30 s), 3 × 150 L2 (15 s) • 100 cool-down **45** min total **20** min L4	• Stationary 5 min warm-up & cool-down • 4 × 30 s sprints 110+ rpm • 4 × 30 s sprints 100 rpm • 4 × 30 s sprints 50-80 rpm 336 watts on all (1:30) **34** min total **7** min L4	
WED			• 10 min warm-up & cool-down • 3 × 400 L2.5-L4 (1 min) • 2 × 800 L2.5-L4 (1 min) • 1 × 1 mile L2.5-L4 (1 min) 7:00 pace on all Hr 173 **50** min total **16** min L4
THURS		• 15 min warm-up • 7-12 × 2 min L4 seated climbs (2 min rest riding back to start) • 15 min cool-down **78** min total **24** min L4	
FRI			• 10 min warm-up • 40 min rolling hills, L1-L2 up, go fast on down parts, 5-10 × 30-60 s • 10 min cool-down **60** min total **0** min L4
SAT	• 300 warm-up • 2-3 × 50, 100, 150, 100, 50 L2.5; 1:57/100 (15 s) • 5 × 100 swim 50/kick 50 (15 s) • 100 cool-down **45** min total **24** min L4	• 1 hr-1 hr 30 min L1 over rolling course, sprint uphill sections **90** min total **10** min L4	
SUN		• 2 hr L1 w/hills **120** min total **20** min L4	
	Total 1:30 **L4** 0:44 48.8%	**Total** 5:22 **L4** 1:01 18.9%	**Total** 1:50 **L4** 0:16 14.5%
	Weekly total 8:42		

Week 3 Bike Emphasis

Monday bike: This is one of those that is more difficult than it reads. Many people find it a long time to be on a stationary bike. The saving factor is that you get to go down in intensity. You will like me for that.

Wednesday bike: This is a fun workout, as well as being a catchall in fitness improvement. You go at an L2.5 level for two minutes. Pedal easy for 30 seconds. Then sprint for 20 seconds, followed by a minute of easy pedaling. Go through this cycle five to eight times, but do fewer if you are starting out. The sprints should be at least 50 watts higher than your L2.5 level.

Wednesday run: I put this in because it is an effective workout. If you haven't been running consistently with some regular intervals, don't do this one. Most of my workouts are interval sessions, not "speed workouts." This one is. Cycling can slow down your leg speed. This insures that it doesn't happen. You run a fast quarter mile and then take as much rest as you want.

Friday bike: If you live in an area with no hills, then flat terrain is fine. A few hills break up a time trial and often can leave you feeling fresher at the end. This is a personal preference. Take it as that.

Saturday swim: These are groups of 3 × 100. The first two are comfortably hard, with 15 seconds between them. After the second one, take a minute, and then swim a 100 as fast as you are able, followed by 30 seconds of peaceful and glorious rest.

	Swim	Bike	Run
MON		• Stationary • 5 min warm-up & cool-down • 3 × 2 min L4+ (3 min) 259 watts • 4 × 2 min L2.5 (2 min) 227 watts • 5 × 2 min L2 (30 s) 191 watts **47** min total **14** min L4	
TUES	• 300 warm-up • 10 × 50 L4 (10 s) 55 s/50 • 10 × 50 sprint 25, easy 25 (15 s) • 300 L2.5 • 150 cool-down **45** min total **25** min L4		
WED		• Stationary • 5 min warm-up & cool-down • 5-8 × [2 min L2.5, 227 watts (30 s) 20 s sprint 300 watts (1 min)] **42** min total **20** min L4	• 10 min warm-up & cool-down • 8-10 × 400 L4+, 92 s/400 (3-5 min walk jog) **60** min total **15** min L4
THURS			
FRI		• 15 min warm-up • 10 mile hilly time trial, L2.5-L4 • 15 min cool-down **60** min total **30** min L4	• 10 min warm-up • 15 min L2 • 5 min L1 • 15 min L2.5 7:18 pace • 10 min cool-down **56** min total **15** min L4
SAT	• 300 warm-up • 5 × [2 × 100 L2.5 (15 s) after 1st, (1 min) after 2nd, 1 × 100 L4+ (30 s)] • 3 × 100 kick (20 s) **50** min total **27** min L4		
SUN		• 2 hr L1 w/hills **120** min total **20** min L4	
	Total 1:35 **L4** 0:52 54.7%	**Total** 4:29 **L4** 1:24 31.2%	**Total** 1:56 **L4** 0:30 25.9%
		Weekly total 8:00	

RUN EMPHASIS

Many people don't improve in running because they always run tired. To improve your running, you need to make sure that you recover enough to feel good during each session. While these weeks each have two consecutive days of running, you may want to alternate weeks so that you run the extra day only every other week. People vary greatly on this. Experiment. By remembering that bike workouts augment your running, you won't be tempted to put in too many miles.

Week 1 Run Emphasis

Tuesday run: If you are starting out, your harder efforts should be just somewhat hard. If you have been running consistently, you may want to go a little faster.

Friday run: The same applies here. Because the time is shorter, you should be running faster than you did in the Tuesday run.

Sunday run: This is a long easy run. The length of it really depends on your recent long runs and race goals. Increase the long run by about 10 percent on alternate weeks until you are at 1 hour and 20 minutes for a 10K run, 2 hours for a half-marathon, and 2 hours and 30 minutes to 3 hours for a marathon.

	Swim	**Bike**	**Run**
MON	• 300 warm-up • 5 × 50 practice rolling (20 s) • 8 × 50, 4 × 100, 1 × 200 L2.5 (20 s) hold 1:57/100 • 4 × 100 kick/swim (15 s) `45` min total `12` min L4	• Stationary • 5 min warm-up • 5 min L1, 5 min L2, 5 min L2.5, 2 min L4 239 watts • 5 min cool-down `30` min total `10` min L4	
TUES			• 10 min warm-up • 3-5 × 5 min L2 (5 min L1) Hr 153 7:36 pace • 10 min cool-down `70` min total `0` min L4
WED			
THURS		• 40 min L1 w/5 × 30 s L4 pickups (complete recovery between) `40` min total `3` min L4	• 45 min L1 `45` min total `0` min L4
FRI			• 10 min warm-up • 5-10 × (2 min L2.5, 2 min L1) • 10 min cool-down `60` min total `20` min L4
SAT	• 300 warm-up • 5 × 100, 50 L1, 50 L2 (25 s) • 15 × 50, 5 × (#1 easy #2 build #3 fast) (15 s) • 5 × 100 L4+ (1:30) `50` min total `20` min L4		
SUN			• 60 min L1 `60` min total `0` min L4
	Total 1:35 **L4** 0:32 33.7%	**Total** 1:10 **L4** 0:13 18.5%	**Total** 3:55 **L4** 0:20 8.5%
		Weekly total 6:40	

Week 1 — Run Emphasis

Week 2 Run Emphasis

A couple of these workouts provide good evaluations of your fitness that can be entered into Performance Progress Plus.

Tuesday swim: You mix strokes on the odd-numbered 50s. Do what you feel like, but do a few that include your least-favorite stroke.

Tuesday run: Keep the rest short on these but run at a fast, repeatable pace. If you begin to lose your pace, take a bonus rest. Then start back a little slower and try again to maintain pace. You can keep increasing the number of these as your fitness level rises. Sixteen is about as much fun as most people can handle.

Wednesday run: The pickups are optional. The whole run is optional. If you are trashed from the day before, don't expect this run to do you any good. If you have recovered, this workout will help to improve your running economy. There is a fine line of recovery here.

Friday swim: The 200s are an excellent fitness indicator. Pay attention to your maintainable pace for these. This time has a very strong correlation to open-water swim performance. Do five 200s if you feel like it. The 75s are a sprint for the first 25 in a nonfreestyle stroke. Then you swim an easy 50 freestyle and rest for 10 seconds.

Friday run: This too is a fitness indicator. You want to run this a little slower than a 10K race pace. The effort will probably rise as you get into the workout. Don't make the common error of running the first mile too fast. Stay fairly comfortable.

Saturday bike: You need to have enough resistance to stand. Some health club bikes won't work for this one. Sit if the bike won't give you something to pedal against. If you are able to stand, try to keep a high cadence. Go through three to five rotations of increasing the standing interval. Most people find a minute challenging.

Week 2 — Run Emphasis

		Swim	Bike	Run
MON			• Stationary • 5 min warm-up • 5-10 × 20 s sprints, try to hold 328 watts (1:30) • 5 min cool-down **30** min total **5** min L4	
TUES		• 300 warm-up • 12 × 50 (mix strokes on odd #s, free on even #s) (20 s) • 6 × 100 build speed on even # laps (20 s) • 150 cool-down **45** min total **20** min L4		• 10 min warm-up • 10-12 × 400 L4 98 s/400 (45 s) Hr 173 • 10 min cool-down **45** min total **19** min L4
WED				• 10 min warm-up • 45 min L1 w/5 × 100 yd pickups, full L1 recovery between **55** min total **0** min L4
THURS				
FRI		• 300 warm-up • 3 × 200 L2.5 (20 s) 1:57/100 • 9 × 75 alt strks 1st lap (10 s) • 4 × 50 kick (20 s) • 150 cool-down **40** min total **10** min L4		• 10 min warm-up • 3-5 × 1 mile L2.5-L4 7:00 pace (45 s-1 min) Hr under 169 • 10 min cool-down **50** min total **30** min L4
SAT			• 5 min warm-up & cool-down • 15 s stand L4, 1 min L1 • 30 s stand L4, 1 min L1 • 1 min stand L4, 1 min L1 **30** min total **9** min L4	
SUN				• 1 hr 20 min L1 Hr 153 8:06 pace **80** min total **0** min L4
		Total 1:25 **L4** 0:30 35.2%	**Total** 1:00 **L4** 0:14 23.3%	**Total** 3:50 **L4** 0:49 21.3%
		Weekly total 6:15		

Week 3 Run Emphasis

Monday run: This should be a fairly steep grade of 8 to 10 percent. The workout is designed to build strength and pushoff. These are hard but not all-out. Watch your effort level. If you sense that you are getting to maximal effort at the top of the hill, back off. This can really beat you up if you do it too hard.

Tuesday bike: Note that there is no rest between effort changes. You just keep going up and down. Time passes quickly on this one.

Thursday run: You will venture into exertional pain on this one. It will build your lactate tolerance and end-of-race spirit. A way to make it more fun is to go out and back on the same route. Turn around halfway through your L1 segment. On your return at L4 try to reach your starting point before 10 minutes. You can stop when you reach the start or 10 minutes, whichever comes first.

Week 3 — Run Emphasis

	Swim	Bike	Run
MON	• 300 warm-up • 5 × 200 L4 (1 min) • 5 × 100 L4 (45 s) 1:48/100 • 5 × 50 L4 (30 S) • 150 cool-down **50** min total **30** min L4		• 10 min warm-up & cool-down • 7-10 × 1 min steep hills L4 Hr under 176 (3:30 with jog down to start) **45** min total **10** min L4
TUES		• Stationary • 5 min warm-up • 5 × [30 s L1, 30 s L2, 30 s L2.5, 1 min L4, 30 s L2.5, 30 s L2, 30 s L1] • 5 min cool-down **30** min total **10** min L4	• 10 min warm-up • 45 min L1 w/5 × 100 yd pickups, full L1 recovery between **55** min total **0** min L4
WED			
THURS			• 10 min warm-up & cool-down • 10 min L4 • 5 min L1 • 10 min L4 6:49 pace Hr under 173 **45** min total **20** min L4
FRI	• 300 warm-up • 3 × 500 at 1,500 m race pace 9:39/500 (1 min) • 4 × 150 kick/swim L2 (20 s) • 150 cool-down **60** min total **24** min L4	• Stationary • 5 min warm-up & cool-down • 5-8 × [2 min L2.5 227 watts (30 s) 20 s sprint 320 watts (1 min)] **42** min total **20** min L4	
SAT			• 10 min warm-up • 50 min rolling hills, L1-L2 up, go fast on down parts • 5-10 × 30-60 s **60** min total **0** min L4
SUN			
	Total 1:50 L4 0:54 49.1%	Total 1:12 L4 0:30 41.6%	Total 3:25 L4 0:30 14.6%
	Weekly total 6:27		

111

	Swim	Bike	Run
MON		• Stationary • 5 min warm-up • 10 × 1 min L4 200 watts (1 min L1) • 5 min cool-down **30** min total **10** min L4	
TUES	• 300 warm-up • 15 × 50 L2.5 (10 s) 56 s • 10 × 50 sprint 25, 25 L1 (15 s) • 5 × 100 kick 50/swim 50 **45** min total **18** min L4		• 10 min warm-up • 10 × 200 ~ 50 s (200 L1) keep running throughout workout • 10 min cool-down **43** min total **8** min L4
WED		• Stationary • 5 min warm-up • 5-10 × 20 s sprint (1:40) 250 watts • 5 min cool-down **30** min total **3** min L4	
THURS			
FRI	• 300 warm-up • 7 × 150 L2.5 (15 s) • 5 × 100 (30 s) odd #s free even #s IM (free 100s are progressive) • 150 cool-down **45** min total **20** min L4		• 10 min warm-up • 35 min L2 **45** min total **0** min L4
SAT		• 2 hr L1 **120** min total **0** min L4	
SUN			• 1 hr L1 Hr 153 8:06 pace **60** min total **0** min L4
	Total 1:30 **L4** 0:38 42.2%	**Total** 3:00 **L4** 0:13 7.2%	**Total** 2:28 **L4** 0:08 5.4%
		Weekly total 6:58	

		Swim	Bike	Run
Week 2 — Balanced Emphasis	**MON**	• 300 warm-up • 5 × 50 practice rolling (20 s) • 8 × 50, 4 × 100, 1 × 200 L2.5 (20 s) hold 1:57/100 • 4 × 100 kick/swim (15 s) 45 min total 12 min L4		
	TUES		• Stationary • 5 min warm-up • 5 min L1, 5 min L2, 5 min L2.5 • 2 min L4 239 watts • 5 min cool-down 30 min total 10 min L4	
	WED	• 300 warm-up • 300 L1 (30 s) 3 × 100 L4 (10 s) • 300 L1 (30 s) 6 × 50 L4 (10 s) • 300 L1 (30 s) 12 × 25 L4 (5 s) • 150 cool-down 50 min total 20 min L4		• 10 min warm-up • 6-8 × 2 min moderate hills L4 (3:30 with jog down to start) • 10 min cool-down 50 min total 16 min L4
	THURS		• 15 min warm-up • 7-12 × 2 min L4 seated climbs (2 min rest riding back to start) • 15 min cool-down 78 min total 24 min L4	
	FRI			
	SAT	• 300 warm-up • 5 × 100, 50 L1, 50 L2 (25 s) • 15 × 50, 5 × (#1 easy #2 build #3 fast) (15 s) • 5 × 100 L4+ (1:30) 50 min total 20 min L4	• 2 hr L1 with 10 min flat L4 in biggest gear you can maintain at 1 hr 30 min 120 min total 10 min L4	
	SUN			• 10 min warm-up • 3-5 × 5 min L2.5-4 (5 min L1) Hr 164 7:18 pace • 10 min cool-down 70 min total 25 min L4
		Total 2:25 L4 0:52 35.9%	Total 3:48 L4 0:44 19.3%	Total 2:00 L4 0:41 34.2%
		Weekly total 8:13		

		Swim	Bike	Run
Week 3 — Balanced Emphasis	**MON**			• 10 min warm-up • 10-12 × 400 L4 98 s/400 (45 s) Hr 173 • 10 min cool-down **45** min total **19** min L4
	TUES		• Stationary • 5 min warm-up • 10-15 × 30 s sprints, try to hold 328 watts (1:30) • 5 min cool-down **40** min total **7** min L4	
	WED	• 300 warm-up • 12 × 50 (mix strokes on odd #s, free on even #s) (20 s) • 6 × 100 build speed on even # laps (20 s) • 150 cool-down **45** min total **20** min L4		
	THURS		• 15 min warm-up • 7-12 × 2 min L4 slight downhill or tailwind 26 mph (3-5 min L1) • 15 min cool-down **63** min total **24** min L4	• 10 min warm-up • 3-5 × 1 mile L2.5-L4 7:00 pace (45 s-1 min) Hr under 169 • 10 min cool-down **50** min total **30** min L4
	FRI			
	SAT	• 300 warm-up • 3 × 200 L2.5 (20 s) 1:57/100 • 9 × 75 alt strks 1st lap (10 s) • 4 × 50 kick (20 s) • 150 cool-down **40** min total **10** min L4	• 30 min L1 • 5 min L4 on flat with no wind • 23 mph avg ? • 50 min L1 **85** min total **5** min L4	
	SUN	• 300 warm-up • 4 × 400 progressive (30 s) • 9 × 75 3 L1, 3 L2, 3 L4 (15 s) • 150 cool-down **50** min total **17** min L4		• 1 hr 20 min L1 Hr 153 8:06 pace **80** min total **0** min L4
		Total 2:15 L4 0:47 34.8%	Total 3:08 L4 0:36 19.1%	Total 2:55 L4 0:49 28%
			Weekly total 8:18	

TIME-HONORED FORM

© Terry Wild Studio

Correcting a form problem is the quickest way to make your training more efficient. Sometimes it's like taking a magic potion. One day you go one pace or speed, and the next you are much faster. The potential for better performance was always there, but poor form held it back. When you learn correct form, nature takes over and you go the pace that you should have all along.

Form correction is part detective work. Quite often, the apparent problem is a compensation for the real problem. Working on the visible part of it is only a Band-Aid. You have to look further for the cure. Once you've found it, you can save years of training time. Sometimes the puzzle is easy to solve. But if you don't get to the root of it all, you will always fall back to the original error.

Good athletic form in all sports is the same thing. You don't learn good form so much as you eliminate unwanted movement. The most fluid and graceful athletes are simply doing less work. All the energy and movement are going directly into the desired job. Awkward movement is extra and wastes energy. This motion away from the task diverts our eye in an unwanted way. That's why it looks bad. Poor form also looks jerky, because muscles are often fighting one another. It's called co-contraction. It would be like trying to bend your arm using the biceps while the triceps fight on the other side of the bone. Human movement is all about muscles pulling on bones. You want to pull on only one side of a bone at a time. The muscle that is not pulling needs to relax. Sometimes if you try too hard, you start working everything at once. We have all probably done that. The muscles that are pulling also need to do so in a straightforward manner, so as not to produce motion in the wrong direction.

Whether it is performing a complex dive, hitting a baseball out of the park, or running a marathon, top performance is produced with little or no wasted motion.

There are common form problems in swimming, cycling, and running that might be holding you back. Your energy should propel you forward, and not much else.

SWIMMING

Water resistance is the problem of the swimmer. Swim form is a strategy of how to use and avoid water's natural thickness and stickiness. Water resistance holds us back, but it also gives us something to grab and pull. You want to create drag as you pull with your arms, but minimize it on your body.

There are all kinds of drag—frictional drag, wave drag, form drag, men with high heels and pearls. I'm a simple guy from a small town, so I don't know much about fashion statements.

Frictional Drag

If you wore a pair of jeans while swimming, you would increase the frictional drag on your legs. The rough surface of the material doesn't slip through the water as skin does. Skin with no hair has less frictional drag than hairy skin, although it probably depends on the initial amount of fur. Wet suits with a smooth surface reduce frictional drag, which is one way they improve swim times. You also ride higher in the water with a wet suit, leaving less surface area in the water and less friction.

Wave Drag

Watch a ship going through the water and you'll notice a big hill of water piling up at the bow. A swimmer's head does the same thing (see figure 7.1). A law of physics applies to anything that moves through the water. It has to do with the length of the vessel and applies to swimmers as small vessels (unless you swim fast enough to plane). The process involves the time it takes the bow wave to pass the boat (or swimmer). Water piles up more quickly on short vessels, thus reducing their hull speed. Longer length at the waterline means a greater speed potential. So a taller person can go faster than a shorter one of equal ability.

An interesting note is that the maximum hull speed for a six-foot vessel is a little faster than the pace of the current 200-meter world record. You can break this law but only for a very short time. You will see a much larger pile of water in front of the head of world-class sprinters as they actually begin to break through it.

Figure 7.1 Note the "bow wave" created by John's head.

Another kind of wave drag is that of the waves themselves. There isn't much you can do about that. Open water is more turbulent than water in a pool protected by lane lines, so depending on how rough it is, your speed potential drops. There is even a noticeable difference in pools with and without lane lines. I've done ocean swims that had much flatter water than a pool with no lane lines.

Form Drag

Form drag is the type of drag over which you have more control. It also has a greater influence on your speed. The dynamics of water and air are quite similar, so many of the same principles apply, with one major difference. Water is 820 times as dense as air. A streamlined position is crucial; you need to present as small an area as possible to the water. Figure 7.2 shows the

Figure 7.2 Paco's whole body has rolled to his left side to create a more streamlined position.

swimmer in a streamlined position. Figure 7.5 is the same swimmer much less streamlined.

Swimming errors that create a side-to-side motion are a common cause of form drag since they increase your frontal area. A part of your body that gets out of alignment creates excess drag. You present a larger area to the water and unwittingly make yourself bigger. And you didn't even get to enjoy the food. A body that stays aligned down a center axis moves through the water faster with no additional effort. There are several ways to get out of alignment.

Overreaching. Overreaching is entering your hand into the water and reaching across your body rather than in front of it. A hand that doesn't pull straight back pulls you to the side. The other hand often overcompensates and pulls you in the opposite direction, producing a snakelike action. First, you need to isolate the lead violator. If you are a one-side breather, watch the hand on that side first. It should reach out directly in front of your shoulder. Then skip a couple of breaths and watch the other side. You may be able to correct an overreaching problem simply by changing your hand entry position. The problem might also stem from head movement. Both arms may be trying to compensate for your shoulders, which follow your head.

Excessive head movement. Excessive head movement is often the cause of other problems. You have a built-in system to keep you going straight. But if you pull yourself to one side, the other side will always have to pull back. If you turn your head too far, you pull your shoulders out of alignment and go to the side to which your head is turning.

You don't need to turn your head any farther than just enough to get a breath (see figure 7.3). The other arm usually

Figure 7.3 John is breathing in a "hole" in the water created by water piling up in front of his head.

makes only a partial compensation. So, if you breathe to the right, theoretically, in a large body of water, you would swim in a big clockwise circle. Practice swimming without breathing for a few strokes and hold your head as steady as you can. When you turn to breathe, think of yourself as still looking forward.

Bilateral breathing can solve this problem. You breathe on both sides with three strokes between breaths. It's a good thing to learn for balanced swimming, although it's not for everyone all the time. People who have been breathing on both sides for years still have a favored side. When you breathe to your favored side, it's easier to stay relaxed. I usually recommend that people learn bilateral breathing for stroke balance, but race in whatever breathing style is most comfortable.

By rolling to each side as you extend your arm, you eliminate the need to turn your head very far when you breathe, you reduce your frontal area, and you eliminate the need to lift your arm high on the recovery. Rolling is a good technique. If you don't roll, you are working too hard. Get a feeling of an exaggerated roll by kicking on your side for five kicks and then rolling to the opposite side for five kicks. Then swim and try to get to the same position on your side. This is more than you need, but you will find the right degree with practice. Your hips and shoulders should roll together.

When you reach out with each arm, roll on to that shoulder with your whole body—hips, feet, the works. This way you present less area to the water. You will also increase your distance per stroke. Another way to think of it is to have your hips roll toward the hand that is finishing the stroke (see figure 7.4).

Early breathing. Sometimes swimmers turn their heads too soon to take a breath. Early breathers often compound the problem by turning their heads too far and lifting them up (see figure 7.5) This creates extra drag on both the chest and shoulders. Early breathers also tend to sink during their breath, which keeps their shoulders lower in the water, also increasing drag. If you breathe on the left side, your head shouldn't turn until the right hand enters the water. Practice getting just a glimpse of the right hand before you take a

Figure 7.4 An underwater view of Paco rolling to his left side. His right hip has rolled toward his right hand as it finishes the stroke.

breath. You want to keep your head motion to a minimum, so don't turn with your chin over your shoulder—turn just enough to get a breath. Inhaling is a good thing, but practice long exhales.

Pulling too wide. Pulling wide is usually a compensation for something happening on the other side. An example might be a right-side breather who pulls the chin way back on the inhale or who breathes too early. This swimmer might pull wide with the left hand to compensate for the upper-body bend caused by the excessive head movement. If you move your head too much, you will slow down.

Trudgen kick. People who were taught to swim in the 1800s learned the trudgen kick, a kind of scissors kick that keeps you from sinking. Sometimes it's just a big kick. The violating leg is usually opposite the breathing side. The big kick buys time

Figure 7.5 Paco presents a much larger surface to the water just by lifting his head and breathing too soon.

to take in more air. As you learn to swim faster, your legs will naturally rise to the surface due to the increased speed, so the need for the trudgen disappears. In the meantime, a trudgen creates drag and slows you down. Practice by swimming short distances at a faster pace than distance swimming, keeping the motion of kick to no more than 14 inches.

Ankle inflexibility. Part of the kicking problem lies in ankle flexibility. If you've come into triathlon from a running background, you may be experiencing a malady I call "runners' disease." Your feet act as if they were nailed to your legs without an ankle. You might even be able to kick backward when trying to go forward. Don't worry; a little improvement will make a big difference.

Ask a friend to help you check your ankle flexibility. Take off your shoes and sit on the floor with your legs extended in front of you. Have your friend measure the distance from the floor to the tip of your tibia (leg bone) just above the ankle at its lowest point. Then point your toes and have your friend measure the distance from the floor to the top of your foot at the end of the metatarsals (foot bones at the base of your toes). Flexible people can point their toes down to the same height as their leg bone. If the difference is more than an inch and a half, you could benefit from more ankle flexibility.

You can improve it just by pointing your toes as you did in the test and then pulling them back as far as you can. Work them back and forth, holding each extreme 5 to 10 seconds. Do this a few times a day and your flexibility and kick will improve.

A swimming kick is not so much a kick at your knee, but a wave of motion initiated at your hip, rolling down your leg like a hose whipped on the driveway on a hot day. As you kick down, the pressure of the water points your toes, and they act like fins finishing your kick. Your foot should be only slightly deeper than your chest at its lowest point.

An ideal position in the water is horizontal, with your heels just barely breaking the surface on the upbeat of each kick. If your feet drag lower than that, you are again increasing you frontal area. The best and fastest way to get a feel for proper position is to use fins. Use them as a tool to experience what a horizontal position feels like. If you rely on them too much, however, you won't want to take them off. Use them for short distances, never for an entire workout. Besides helping with position in the water, the fins also help to develop greater ankle flexibility.

All aspects of correct swimming form tend to work together. By taking less time on the inhale, you don't need the trudgen kick. By not turning your head too far, you won't need to pull wide to straighten yourself out. If you don't overreach, you will swim with less effort. You will be in less of a panic to breathe. By going faster you will decrease your dependence on the trudgen. With these small corrections you will begin to swim faster. As your speed increases, these things will also tend to correct themselves. The faster you go, the faster you go.

With drag reduced, you should go farther as you pull yourself over the bottom. If you take the same number of strokes each minute but get more distance with each one, you will go faster. It's simple. You want to get as much distance per stroke as possible up to a point. If you exaggerate your distance per stroke you will begin to slow down. And if you try to go faster simply by whipping your arms as fast as possible, you will slow down. Aim for a happy medium between the two.

Everyone is a little different. It's a lot like cycling cadence. Some people push big gears with a slower cadence, and some spin. You have to find what is right for you and then improve it. Once you get your distance per stroke up to 1.3 yards, or 1.2 meters (19 strokes per 25-yard lap, 21 strokes per 25-meter lap), then turning over faster is probably your best bet for gaining speed. But if you can't get at least a yard per stroke, your arms aren't getting a grip on the water. Here is an example. If you can get 1.3 yards per stroke and 65 strokes per minute, then you can swim 1,500 meters in just over 19 minutes (1.3 yards × 65 strokes per minute = 84.5 yards per minute = 77.3 meters per minute; 1,500 meters ÷ 77.3 = 19.40 minutes). If you can get 1.3 yards per stroke with 60 strokes per minute, your time would be just over 21 minutes. This 1.3 yards-per-stroke swimmer would do well to increase turnover for more speed. If you get only 0.9 yards per stroke with 60 strokes per minute, your time would be 30 minutes. You should work on increasing your distance per stroke. The Performance Progress Plus swimming program can calculate these numbers for you.

What Is Good Swimming?

I've covered swimming problems first, because form is a crucial element of performance, and using correct form will save training time. I've had people make huge improvements in a matter of days with form corrections. But enough about problems. Even if you have no major problems, here are some things that can help.

Sometimes drag is a good thing. Unlike your body, your hands and arms should have as much drag as possible. They are what grabs the water, so you want to minimize the slip. It would be great if you could grow arm hair at the beginning of each stroke and then shed it during recovery. If you can't do that, you need to maximize your pulling surface. As you are beginning your stroke, you want to rotate your upper arm inward so that your elbow stays high. You can try this as you are reading. Just extend your arm straight out from your shoulder and pull your hand back without moving your upper arm. Now try it again. This time as you begin to pull back, rotate your upper arm inward. See how your elbow stays high? Also look at your forearm. With your upper arm rotated inward, your forearm is at a much steeper angle to the floor as you pull back. In the water, in this position, it presents a much larger surface area to the water and greater form drag. This means more distance per stroke.

As you do this underwater you want to keep your palm facing backward during the entire pulling process. This movement has been described as "reaching over the barrel" (see figure 7.6). It must be an old comparison because you don't see many barrels around these days. In any case, when your elbow begins to drop during the pull, your arm slips.

Figure 7.6 John's left arm is just beginning to "reach over the barrel."

Finding your stroke and kick timing. For simplicity, let's say that you swim at 60 strokes per minute, which is one stroke cycle every two seconds. Although you should have one stroke per second, it may be slightly imbalanced, which means that one arm is always playing catch-up. This creates a "limp" in your stroke. When this occurs, there is often a compensation with the foot that causes one wide or long kick: a modified trudgen as explained earlier. That big kick puts your foot outside the streamlined zone created by your body. And rather than being propulsive, it becomes a braking and balancing kick. This cycle of starting and stopping is extremely common, even in seasoned swimmers.

One of the biggest reasons for an interrupted stroke cycle is our love for air. I'll admit it. I've developed a habit of breathing air every day. When we exercise, we need more. But just as important as inhaling oxygen is exhaling carbon dioxide. It is not a lack of oxygen that gives us an elevated breathing drive. It is the buildup of carbon dioxide.

When we have this elevated breathing drive, we tend to take longer inhales. Instead, we should be taking longer exhales to blow off the carbon dioxide. A right-side breather with a long inhale will lie on the left arm. The arm must wait for you to finish savoring your inhale before it can get to the business of pulling you through the water. The right arm then has less time to finish the cycle, and the left foot might kick wide. In this case, you need to concentrate on longer exhales and shorter inhales. Get your face back in the water sooner, and your left arm will respond with an earlier "catch."

In a balanced stroke, there is a propulsive kick with the beginning of each arm stroke. It begins when your arm has pulled back about a foot, or 10 degrees of rotation, and it ends at about 30 degrees of rotation (see figure 7.7). Synchronizing your stroke and kick can cure as many ills as maintaining a steady head. Stroke and kick timing is often the original and unseen problem, causing a whole cascade of compensations. If nothing else, proper synchronization will keep your feet aligned behind your body.

Some people will make three kicks with each arm stroke, or six kicks when you count both legs. This is called a six-beat kick. Other people kick four times, and still others two.

Figure 7.7 Karen's right leg has just begun its downward movement.

It doesn't really matter, because the only kick that is propulsive is the one coordinated with the arm stroke. The rest are balance kicks. In distance swimming, the kick provides only about 30 percent of the propulsion, so you don't have to be a great kicker, just one who can keep your feet behind your body.

I've found that it is easier to stay in alignment if you can learn to accentuate the propulsive kick on each side. If you naturally have a two-beat kick, everything is fine. If you have a six-beat or four-beat kick, try doing two-beat kick catch-up drills to learn the emphasis kick (see figure 7.8). The catch-up drill can help not only with kick timing but also with learning to roll. Practice rolling your hips toward the hand that is finishing the stroke. One-arm swimming is also good for practicing rolling and achieving a strong finish to the stroke.

Figure 7.8 Karen holds her right hand in front until the left hand "catches" up to it.

CYCLING

It's hard to look bad on a bike. The form considerations of cycling are subtle positioning changes that can increase your power. The scenarios of unseen problems and compensations don't exist here. If you have a problem, it's often not noticeable.

An efficient pedal stroke, like an efficient swimming stroke, is a very refined movement, but the process of learning it is different. In swimming, you have to think about what you are doing to make corrections. In cycling, because your foot can only go around in circles, you learn just by doing it. You don't have to think at all. You just have to avoid taking wrong turns and hitting things.

The refinement in the pedal stroke is in coordinating your glutes (butt), your quads, and your calves to produce maximum power at just the right time. You improve this in part with more cycling, because it is a neural response that requires learning. As in swimming, maximum power is determined by your joint angles, which rely on positioning on the bike.

Where to Sit

Where you sit is the most important consideration in cycling form. It is fore-and-aft positioning that can have the largest impact. Small changes fore-and-aft will create much larger joint-angle changes than moving the saddle up or down. The angle between your upper body and torso and the angle at the knee are what determine your power output.

You want to take advantage of the maximum of force and speed generated at the hip and the knee. But there is give-and-take in both directions.

A smaller angle at the hip (more bent over) allows greater force but reduces cadence.

Hip

Your upper leg has a dramatic speed change as it goes through a pedal cycle. It accelerates as it moves down in the pedal stroke. The more open your hip angle, the faster your leg moves and the faster your cadence. As you move forward in the saddle, you open your hip angle. If you slide back, you close it down. Hip extension is a much more forceful action when the angle between your torso and upper leg is small. But the smaller the angle gets, the slower the movement. This kind of position is good for hills, except that most people like to sit up for easier breathing. Sliding back in the saddle accomplishes both. A more open angle at the hip (forward position) allows for faster cadence at the expense of force. So you want to be forward in a tailwind, on the flats, or on slight downgrades. The angle at which there is an optimum of the two is about 60 degrees between the torso and upper leg. The rider in figure 7.9 gives a good example of this position. At an angle less than 60 degrees, the speed decreases. In wider angles, the force begins to diminish.

Figure 7.9 Edgar's hip is at a 60 degree angle and his knee at 110 degrees when his right foot is in the "power zone."

Knee

Peak power at the knee occurs at about 110 degrees. In a proper setup, the optimum joint angles should coincide as the crank arm is horizontal and forward in the "power zone." Also at this point, your knee should be directly over the pedal spindle. Again, the rider in figure 7.9 gives a good example. This position is time honored and well proven. But where you are sitting relative to the bike will vary with the ratio of your upper to lower leg.

Most people have an upper leg that is slightly longer than the lower part. A common ratio is 1.1 to 1. To find your ratio, first measure from the big bump at your hip to the upper bump on the outside of your knee. That's your femur length. Next, measure from the lower bump on the inside of your knee to the big bump on the inside of your ankle. That's the length of your tibia. The ratio is the femur length divided by the tibia length. If it is less than 1.1, you should be set up forward on the bike.

If your ratio is over 1.1 and you like to time trial at slower cadences with big gears, you might prefer a position slightly more aft, where it is generally easier to maintain force. People with a ratio of over 1.15 will have a fairly open angle at the hip, and so can sit still farther back. Think of your lower leg as a prop for the upper. A shorter prop doesn't hold your knee as high, resulting in a more open angle to the torso. If people with a shorter lower leg move too far forward, they throw the power phase of their pedal stroke out of synch.

Personal preference plays a role. If you like to push big gears at a cadence in the 80s or lower, then a rear seating position is for you. There is nothing wrong with this kind of cycling. You may even be able to ride slightly faster pushing a big gear and sitting back. But slow-cadence gear mashing can slow down your running. If you can go 30 seconds faster on the bike but slow your run by two minutes, you're down a minute and a half. If you feel that it is easier to generate power at a higher cadence, then a more forward position is best. Most people will find it easier to run after riding at a higher cadence in a more forward position. For hills, however, your saddle adjustment should still allow you to move back.

Also pay attention to your position in aero bars. Most people tend to close down their hip angles when going to an aero position. You will probably want to move forward to open that angle slightly.

---

*M*any people find that they can produce more power by tilting their pelvis toward the ground. This will arch the lower back and increase power.

Form Problems

Many cycling inefficiencies are the result of not learning to relax. With a proper setup for positioning, the bike should almost feel like a part of you. Even with that, sometimes people just fight too hard.

Rigid arms (locked elbows). When riding with your hands on the brake hoods or drops, you should keep your arms relaxed. Riding with elbows locked and arms rigid is dangerous. People take nasty falls because they react to a small object in the road by pulling on the bars. A crash will really cost you some training time. As long as the front wheel is heading forward, a bike will stay up on its own until it stops. For those who like fancy words, a bike has gyroscopic stability. It doesn't want to fall down. If your arms stay relaxed, the front wheel will keep heading down the road and the rest will follow.

Holding your arms rigid also takes work. On a bike, your legs are supposed to do all the work. If your arms aren't working, more energy is available for your legs.

Choppy pedal stroke (pounding the pedals). You want to be turning the pedal throughout 360 degrees. You slide forward at the top, push down in the front, pull back at the bottom, and pull up at the back. Sometimes people will push down with the leg that they should be pulling up. Get the feeling that you are pedaling in circles.

Slow cadence. The problem with a slow cadence is that you are probably in too big a gear. By pushing so much harder you build up lactic acid sooner, and you will then probably have to slow down to clear it. Pushing a big gear will also slow down your run time during a race. There are people who will tell you to push the biggest gear you can, and there are people who will say spinning is the answer. What they do may work for them but not for you. Try both extremes and find what works. Always keep in mind that in a triathlon you must also run.

Inability to stand in hills. It's best to decide whether to sit or stand on a hill while you are climbing it. It usually works out that you will do both. You can climb standing in one gear higher than you can sitting. Standing gives you more options, and you use different muscle groups in the two styles. If you don't know how to stand, practice on a level street first. There is a tendency to stand too far back. You want to have your weight forward over the bars and learn to subtly rock the bike back and forth as you pedal.

Aerodynamics versus comfort. This is a give-and-take situation. You will read many magazine articles about the most aerodynamic position, bike, helmet, and so forth. Everything down to socks has been tested in a wind tunnel. But the rider produces nearly 80 percent of the wind drag, so the largest factor is your position on the bike. Aerodynamic socks won't help. The use of aero bars, however, can reduce your wind drag by 25 percent. The catch is that the most aerodynamic position may not accommodate the most efficient pedaling. Your hip angle may be closed too much, or you simply may not be comfortable. If you aren't comfortable you won't ride as fast and will fatigue sooner. It's better to position yourself a little higher if it gives you greater comfort. Remember that the people in the wind tunnels aren't going anywhere, and they don't have to run after they get out.

RUNNING

Running is the most natural of the three triathlon sports. No one had to teach you how to run the first time you tried. It just happened. And then you fell. Through trial and error you developed your own style and learned not to fall. Running styles are like a signature or set of fingerprints. There are parts of it that you can't change, no matter how hard you try. A local running club has comedians who parody each other's running style. It always gets a laugh, but only partly because of the intended humor. It's hard to run like someone else, and it usually doesn't come out right.

Running has a consideration that doesn't play in cycling or swimming. There is a flight from which you land (see figure 7.10). Landing uses energy that is then unavailable to move you forward. This is why heavier people sometimes don't like running as much. They spend a greater percentage of their energy just staying erect. Everything you do in the other sports should somehow propel you forward.

Form Problems

Little can be done to correct running form. A few tendencies, however, can detract from running economy, a topic that we cover in the next chapter. And in running, we get back to the situation of unseen problems producing visible compensations.

Figure 7.10 Jonathan has to land from this flight pattern every stride. The faster you go, the higher and farther you fly.

Overstriding. Taking excessively big steps is the most common problem that I see. Most recreational runners overstride. Young runners overstride like crazy. I think it starts from thinking that if you want to go faster, you have to reach out and grab more real estate, as you do in the pool. But it doesn't work as well on land. If your foot is out in front of your center of gravity as it lands, you slow down. Because it's so far out in front, the foot has to stop to let the rest of you catch up. The brakes are on. You use more energy to absorb the landing impact. It's trouble all around, because overstriding can lead to injuries.

An extreme heel-first landing is a sign of overstriding (see figure 7.11). The only way that you can get your foot out that far is to land way back on your heel. Look at yourself running in front of a store window; or better yet, look at yourself on

Figure 7.11 Catherine's right foot is landing in front of her center of gravity and creates a braking effect.

videotape. You want your foot to be directly underneath your knee as your weight comes down.

Most people who overstride are running too upright. Their bodies are perpendicular to the ground (see figure 7.11). In effect, they are running in front of their center of gravity, which is more of a pulling stride than a pushing one. People who run this way also tend to bounce up and down.

Envision your head traveling from point A to point B over a race course. If it goes in a straight line, it travels a shorter distance than if it has to go up and down. Vertical running directs energy away from the line that you want to take. It is uneconomical. You work harder and have to go farther.

You want to have the sensation that you are pushing off from behind. Some people sense that they have longer contact with the ground. This is what you want. You are then putting some stretch on your Achilles tendon, which will improve your running economy. Others say that it feels more like pushing than pulling. Many people don't like it at first. It feels different. But they run faster and easier without a fitness change when it becomes natural.

To get a sense of the position, I often will grab someone by the shirt and pull them into an extreme forward-leaning position. (You should see the looks of surprise.) You should lean forward from the feet to the head. You don't want to bend at the waist. To start, practice running in an excessive forward lean for about 20 yards. Visualize some wise guy pulling you by your shirt. Then try a more moderate lean for about a minute of running. You should be about three to five degrees forward. It is important to bring your hips forward with your chest. You can't change your running form right away; your style is too ingrained. It's best to practice the forward lean with short pickups or in 200-meter repeats.

I've found that the remaining form problems, though relatively minor, will also prevent you from running efficiently.

Imbalanced arm swing.   If your arms aren't swinging evenly, then most likely your upper body is twisting. This is a sideways motion that won't propel you forward. You are compensating for something. Usually the problem is not your arm. Your arm is probably compensating for back tightness. The first thing that you want to check is your lower-back flexibility. Sit down with your legs extended in front and your feet about a foot apart. Reach toward your feet with your hands together. If you can't reach beyond your heels you have a tight back and hamstrings. Try doing some stretching exercises for your back and hamstrings, and after a few weeks your arm swing should even out.

Tight shoulders.   Tight shoulders create a hunched look. You might begin to have difficulty hearing because your shoulders are in your ears. Nearly everyone does it as they begin to fatigue. It tends to make your arm swing choppy, which translates to the legs and produces a choppy stride. It takes more effort to maintain a choppy stride. Periodically take a few breaths with a slightly different rhythm and let your shoulders drop. It also helps to relax your jaw, which works down to the shoulder, to the arms, and finally to the legs. If you work at a desk, you should do the same thing during your work day.

Bent at the waist (sitting in a bucket).   This happens when you try to learn a forward lean and don't bring your hips forward. It's much more difficult to run bent over. Try it in an extreme position, like running under a low branch. You can feel muscles working against gravity, because you have moved your center of gravity out in front of your feet. If you straighten up and pull your hips forward, you suddenly feel lighter. Your weight is over your feet.

Choppy breathing patterns.   We think of breathing as the singular function of taking in oxygen. But we also exhale carbon dioxide. As we accumulate lactic acid in our blood during exercise, we exhale carbon dioxide to buffer it. If you are taking short, choppy breaths you are probably getting all the oxygen you need, but you are inhibiting this buffering process by not exhaling enough carbon dioxide. Short breathing also has a tendency to tighten you up. Breathing patterns should have a long full exhale before inhaling. You want to feel your diaphragm working as you breathe. This is called "belly breathing." It's an easy thing to forget when you fatigue. Part of the problem is that your breathing muscles fatigue just as your legs do. You need to practice full breathing all the time so that the endurance capacity of those muscles increases along with that of your legs.

Form corrections of any kind can forge rapid changes. The hard part is that the longer you have been doing something, the more readily you will fall back into an old form habit. Motor learning is a repetitive process. The more you repeat something, the better you learn it. Old dogs can learn new tricks; it just takes them longer.

TIMELY
TUNE-UPS AND
QUICK FIXES

© Richard Etchberger

There are a few tricks that can improve your performance. Along with form corrections, these can put a little more snap in what you do and add little or no training time. Tune-ups and quick fixes are not like those we discussed in chapter 1. They are metabolic changes. Tune-ups and quick fixes are more like form corrections and come under the category of motor learning. You teach your body how to respond to certain situations. You then learn the most efficient muscle recruitment to get the job done. You have to think about some of these things at first, but once you learn any of them, the actions are unconscious. The result is you get more for less. Top performers come by this naturally without ever giving it a thought. It's a part of what being a natural athlete is all about. The rest of us might want to consider a few things.

SWIMMING POWER

Once your swimming form is relatively correct, you can then add more power to your stroke, and get more speed. I say relatively correct, because no one has a perfect stroke. Getting the most out of your stroke, whatever it is, becomes time-saving swimming.

Emphasizing the Pull and the Push

An emphasis in your stroke can come from the pull, early in the stroke, or from the push, late in the stroke. A textbook stroke is one in which your hand accelerates from start to finish. Your hand produces the greatest power as it pushes from approximately your abdomen to your hip. The main muscles you are recruiting are the triceps. This is fine if you have powerful triceps. But not everyone is blessed with big, strong arms. Because the triceps are a relatively small muscle group, lactic acid quickly builds up to the point of discomfort. When you begin to fatigue, your stroke becomes shorter. You don't push through as hard or as fast or as far. Usually turnover remains about the same, but the distance per stroke diminishes and your speed drops.

The pulling part of the stroke is from the lats. They are big slabs of muscle on your back that attach to your upper arm.

Because lats are such large muscles, you can recruit more fibers to get the job done. In chapter 1 we discussed muscle recruitment being related to lactate buildup. Larger muscles pull with more fibers. They can create more power with less recruitment relative to the overall muscle mass. They don't have to recruit as many fast-twitch muscle fibers. With a greater percentage of slow-twitch fibers being recruited, lactic acid is metabolized rather than accumulated. When your arm is out in front in the early part of the stroke, you use your lats to pull it back. In open-water swimming, it makes sense for many people to emphasize the pull and not push quite as hard.

In group settings, I sometimes do a drill in which everyone first swims with a pushing emphasis. Next, they relax the push and swim with more of a pull. When put to a vote, about 70 percent (a conservative estimate) favor a pulling emphasis. The times will generally be faster, and the effort easier, when they swim with the favored emphasis. So while some will push, more will pull. In a triathlon, it is important to finish the swim still feeling fresh. If you are excessively fatigued from the swim, your bike leg suffers. If your bike leg suffers, your run goes straight to the trash. There can be a snowball effect of fatigue beginning in the water. In an international distance race, a swim in which you pushed yourself for a minute faster time can cost your 5 to 10 minutes on the bike and run. Sometimes you try too hard and get slower.

An elite sprinter needs to recruit all fibers at once, both pulling and pushing. More is better, and lactate accumulation is not an issue. Distance swimmers, on the other hand, need to be able to maintain a pace. Efficient recruitment patterns can make a difference.

The way to maintain your pace is to accent your specialty or strength. You can find it by swimming a set of 50s or 100s with no more than 20 seconds of rest. You have to exaggerate the different parts of the stroke to see a difference. First do the push. Begin your stroke with a minimum pull and make big accelerations from your chest to your thigh. Do a few repeats like that. Take a little break, and then try the pull. Concentrate on reaching out as far as you can. Roll on the shoulder of the outstretched arm, and pull back hard to about your chest.

Then ease up to finish your stroke at about the hip. This is what happens in a fatigued stroke. But in that state, there usually isn't much of a pull either. After a few repeats, you will know which method you like best. Become familiar with both and change it around during your workouts. There is no question that a perfect stroke is a combination of the push and pull. For those who aren't perfect, emphasizing either the push or the pull is usually an improvement.

Increasing Stroke Distance or Turnover

In the last chapter, I touched on the subject of turnover versus distance per stroke. It all gets back to the original concept of power and finding the optimum blend of speed and force. Everyone is a little different, so you have to choose an avenue. Once you reach a reasonably good measure for distance per stroke, the force component, you should try to move your arms faster. This is the quickest way to improve performance. If you have a fast turnover, then you need to have a longer stroke.

I've found 19 strokes per 25 yards, or 21 strokes for 25 meters, to be a reasonably good distance per stroke for regular people. It's not time efficient to train for more distance per stroke. A performance improvement will come more quickly by learning to pull your stroke distance faster. Move your arms faster. During a swim emphasis phase, you would want to spend a couple of days a week with some form of sprinting—either 25s or 50s or even a set with half-lap sprints (see swim emphasis tables in chapter 6). This simply teaches your arms to move faster. Practice throwing them out quickly for the next stroke. Then it becomes a matter of sustaining the extra speed. To make a significant difference in an open-water distance swim, you need to maintain a speed increase up to 200 yards (meters). A repeatable time for that distance will indicate your open-water pace. Better swimmers who have hit a plateau can benefit from increased speed work.

The other side of this business is pertinent if you are over 20 strokes for 25 yards, or 22 for 25 meters. Regardless of your turnover, you need more distance per stroke. I've worked with one swimmer who can get his arms moving at 100 strokes per minute for a sprint. But he gets only three-quarters of a meter per stroke for those efforts. Part of that is his natural strategy. But his improvement is all coming through increasing distance per stroke. Working on stroke and kick timing with catch-up drills has made a big difference. Another part of his stroke strategy is that he is a pusher. This is due in part to naturally tight shoulders that interfere with his reaching out. But little by little, his shoulders are becoming more flexible. He has also improved his stroke distance by rolling. As his distance per stroke increases, his times drop. He doesn't need more arm speed; he needs more of a stroke in the initial stages. So he has both speed and force but not for the entire stroke. Weights or resistance exercises won't help him as much as increasing his shoulder and arm flexibility.

Still other swimmers will have high arm turnover but a weak pull or push. Sprint sets one or two days per week help these people develop more force by using total muscle recruitment. When this sort of person sprints, they should concentrate on a hard pull and push rather than high turnover. Resistance exercises will help increase the force of the arm movement.

CYCLING POWER

On a bicycle, force and distance collectively come from gear inches, which produce the distance traveled with each pedal stroke. Bigger gears require more force and cover more distance. But pushing a big gear won't do you any good if you pedal at a cadence of only 40. Cadence is the speed component. Some people are better at generating power with a slower cadence and big gears, and some people are better spinners. Professional riders tend to spin more during road races or criteriums, but grind big gears when time trialing. It all boils down to how many watts you can produce. Watts are a power measure (a product of force and speed). You can convert watts to horsepower, but no one would like the number. Three hundred watts is a lot of power—25 mph on flat ground in still air—but it is only four-tenths of one horsepower. Who wants to be four-tenths of anything? So watts are slowly becoming the standard of evaluating cycling performance. Most people can keep a 75-watt lightbulb burning without too much trouble. Until affordable bike computers can measure watts, table 8.1 will

Table 8.1 — Power Equivalents

Speed (mph)	Aero bars		Drop bars	
	Watts	Calories/hr	Watts	Calories/hr
15	69	332	83	379
18	109	475	130	552
20	165	680	197	798
22	200	809	238	948
23	228	912	272	1,073
24	260	1,029	310	1,213
25	294	1,154	350	1,360
26	330	1,286	394	1,521
27	370	1,433	441	1,694
28	413	1,591	492	1,881
29	459	1,760	547	2,083
30	508	1,940	605	2,296

give you equivalents to make power comparisons and chart improvement. Performance Progress Plus can do this for you.

To go faster, you need to pedal faster and push a bigger gear. Faster and bigger equals power.

Part of your sustained power comes from the same muscle enzymes that enhance oxygen consumption and raise lactate threshold. So, to a degree, there is a training overlap to increase all these functions. All training is good for you. But to isolate power training and save time, you need to train the nerves that fire the muscles. For some people, changes from neural training come very quickly. In part, this results from learning to pedal smoothly in "circles." I believe that the larger part of power increase, however, lies in a very refined recruitment of your glutes, hamstrings, quads, and solei (calves). They all come into play at just the right moment in an efficient pedal stroke. Studies have demonstrated that power is produced in a range of 10 to 15 degrees where the crank arm is horizontal and forward (see figure 8.1). So even though you want to create a smooth pedal stroke, you develop power when you push down on the pedals, just like the first time you rode your trike. The rest of the stroke cycle is getting ready for the power phase. Smooth pedaling occurs when your legs don't fight each other. When you pull up, you are assisting the leg that is pushing down by unweighting the recovering leg. You produce very little power from pulling up on the pedals. All you have to do is learn to push harder and faster and stay relaxed.

Finding Power in Speed

The quick way to build power is through sprint efforts of 20 to 30 seconds. It may not sound like much, and on paper it looks the same, but the 10 extra seconds are big ones. You don't start to accumulate lactic acid until 20 seconds into an effort. In a

Figure 8.1   The crank arm is in the "power zone."

short sprint, lactate buildup occurs rapidly. By the time you get to 30 seconds, your power has probably dropped. So start with 20-second sprints at a level about 10 percent higher than your maximal aerobic capacity. Later, as you can generate higher power outputs for 20 seconds, try to hold your original level for 30 seconds. Table 8.1 will give you conversions from miles per hour on the road to watts or calories per hour. Some health club stationary bikes will give a display of calories per hour. If you are at maximal aerobic capacity at 300 watts, your sprints should be around 330 watts. Performance Progress Plus can give you your watts at $\dot{V}O_2$ max. If you don't know your maximum, a sprint is a higher power output than you could maintain for a minute.

Sprint workouts are one of greatest time-saving devices I know. On a stationary bike, most people find that 30 minutes is plenty. Your cadence during these wattage episodes should be well over 100.

Muscle recruitment order is learned in training. If you only train at 80 rpm, your recruitment order will be geared to that leg speed. Anything faster will turn that order into chaos. In essence, your muscle fibers cease being good soldiers working together, and become an angry mob fighting itself. It's a lot of energy going nowhere. When you practice these sprints, you get a full recovery between so that you can tell people how much fun you're having.

Finding Power in Force

As long as you are training with high cadence sprints, you can then build force through low cadence, high resistance sprints.

You can also build force with hill repeats of one to two minutes. Do them in a seated position so that you use and strengthen your glutes (butt muscles). The glutes will help you maintain your speed on the flats. To really learn to handle resistance, occasionally do hill repeats in one gear higher than your preferred gear for the climb.

During a cycling phase, devote one day per week to sprints and one day to hill repeats. Two days of resistance exercises are the most time efficient. The sprints are better on the stationary bike, and the whole workout can take less than 40 minutes. The large amount of power and high cadence will teach your muscles to fire efficiently. The power workouts will force them to do so. Remember that your body will do only as much as you ask it to do.

Once you are able to repeat a given wattage or power output, you might want to test yourself to see what you can maintain for five minutes at just under threshold. If it is higher than what you have been able to do before, then the power workouts have paid off.

---

*N*ow start working on extending your time at your new threshold power. The goal is really to learn to hold more power for a longer period.

Whatever your sustained power level, it will be easier to maintain if you alter your efforts. Trying to put the hammer down and hold it will get you tired. Experiment with going easier for 30 seconds every few minutes, or with doing one easier pedal stroke every four or five strokes. You need to give your legs a chance to remove the lactic acid, and intermittent easier efforts will do that.

RUNNING ECONOMY

In running, while maximal oxygen consumption is a big part of who wins races, less oxygen consumption at a less-than-maximal pace is just as big a factor. Maybe bigger. Running economy is like that of an automobile. It is a comparison of energy consumption at an equal effort. In cars we use gasoline usage as the measure; in the human body we use oxygen consumption.

Two cars racing at the same speed may use different amounts of fuel. Late in the race, the more economical car still has gas and can maintain or accelerate the pace. A less economical car may run out of fuel. Remember, we said in chapter 1 that you first recruit slow-twitch fibers, and as you speed up, you recruit more fast-twitch fibers. An economical runner is probably recruiting fewer fibers to run the same speed. That means there are fewer fast-twitch fibers recruited early in the race. Late in the race, when the runner needs them, they are fresh, and a less economical runner has already fatigued them and is beginning to slow down. Economical runners are those who don't fade late in a race. If your running pace fades, read on.

Consistent research has shown that running economy plays an important role in performance. Unfortunately, no one has yet been able to define specifically what contributes to running economy. Like overuse injuries, running economy develops over a long time and has multiple contributors. You can't pin it on one thing. You can learn to improve parts of your running economy in a single session. Other parts you learn over years. Because this is a book about saving time, we'll look at the easier answers.

Economy From Muscle Elasticity

There is an elastic component in muscles and tendons that contributes to economy. If you take a muscle fiber and stretch it, it will snap back like a rubber band. It's an action that doesn't require oxygen or fuel. It's a free ride. When your leg is stretched out behind you, and your heel is on the ground, there is a slight stretch on your calf muscles and Achilles tendon, just before pushoff. An economical pushoff is one that lets this very subtle elasticity assist the muscle before it shortens. This elasticity also helps your leg spring through the recovery rather than pull through it. Again, it's a free ride.

Hill running is good for developing strength for the pushoff as well as lengthening the Achilles tendon. Use hills of varying pitch. Do shorter repeats up steep hills and longer repeats on more moderate hills. While there is more Achilles stretch on a steep hill, your running mechanics are far different from flat running. Moderate grades offer a compromise.

Economy From the Footfall

The landing is another part of running that affects economy. If your foot comes down harder than necessary, you create extra work. This work, unfortunately, gets you nowhere, although it does keep your knees and face off the pavement. Running involves a flight phase in your stride, and flying of any form requires a landing. (Gravity always wins.) You should learn to land lightly with a more forward lean. To do that, you must strengthen the muscles that absorb the impact. One way to strengthen your landing gear is through fast downhill running for short distances. As your landing muscles get stronger, you reduce the need for extra recruitment. Less recruitment is what defines economy. Rolling hills with a gentle grade, as shown in figure 8.2, is a good place to try this. Running emphasis week 3 in chapter 6 includes a downhill running workout. Before doing this kind of training, be aware that it can be hard on knees, ankles, and back. A couple of days a month are usually plenty.

More Economy Tips

Economy seems to be specific to race distance. A recent study of elite runners by Jack Daniels, PhD, a key researcher on running economy, showed that at faster speeds, shorter

Figure 8.2 Pick a hill not too steep like this one to practice downhill running.

distance specialists (up to 10K) were more economical than elite marathoners. At slower speeds, the marathoners were more economical. That tells you either that these runners chose particular race distances because of inborn economy or that race-specific training and racing made them economical at their distances. This is where racing and tempo runs come into the training picture. If you race once or twice a month at a 10K or shorter distance, you'll probably find yourself getting faster as long as you are doing your other training. You might just be improving your economy at these distances. If nothing else, you'll still get faster through threshold changes. This also tells you that doing the miles necessary for marathon training most likely won't help in training for a 10K.

Stride Distance or Turnover?

Over a 10K course, most triathletes will take over eight thousand steps. I could probably live without this information. Nevertheless, since I've opened this can of worms, I suppose we should address it. Should you take more or fewer strides?

Your size and running ability determine your optimal stride rate and distance. Some runners should take fewer steps; some should take more. You might just find that your optimal stride rate falls in line with your bike pedaling cadence.

Jack Daniels has found that stride rates of elite runners are about the same. So stride distance is the major factor that determines speed differences. If you count the stride rate of elite distance runners, you will find that most of them will run at 90 to 95 strides per minute. A 5:00-mile pace at this rate requires a stride distance of 170 centimeters between footfalls. A faster runner in this caliber will find the way to faster times by soaring an extra 5 centimeters. (They really fly.) At that stride rate, it's tough to get your legs to move much faster. Try it if you don't believe me. The extra 5 centimeters would increase the pace to 4:50, or just over a minute in a 10K.

A number of cycling studies have demonstrated that at high power output, elite riders prefer a cadence of 90 to 100. Are you seeing a pattern develop? There is actually less oxygen cost to produce a given wattage in a higher gear at a lower cadence. This style of pedaling is more economical. But cycling performance, unlike running, has nothing to do with economy. The extra force needed makes it seem more difficult. If it seems more difficult, then there is an increased lactate buildup. Unless you enjoy pain, you will do what it takes to make it easier. Shift down and pedal faster.

So a turnover that successful legs seem to enjoy, in both cycling and running, is around 90 to 95 times per minute. OK, that's great for elite runners and cyclists, but how does that affect the rest of us? Most of us don't possess the genetic equipment to maintain a 5:00-mile pace for more than a sprint. In a very general sense, most people that I've coached have benefited from increasing their turnover. Overstriding, a very common problem, will cause a slow turnover and is uneconomical. Without any stride counting or pace watching, there is a good probability that you will benefit from a shorter stride and higher turnover.

Knowing that a 10K requires 8,000 steps may not be useful, but it's helpful to know your stride rate. You shouldn't be running any slower than 85 strides per minute. Just as in swimming, however, there is a point at which distance per stride becomes more important. Your leg length also factors in. If you are five-feet-two-inches, I doubt that you can maintain a stride distance of 170 centimeters. That's a long flight for anyone. Catherine, for example, gets 140 centimeters at 100 strides for a 5:45 pace. If Jonathan, on the other hand, is six-feet-four-inches, it will probably be difficult for him to run at a turnover rate of 100 strides per minute. Jonathan runs a 5:45 pace at 90 strides per minute, even though his running style is similar to Catherine's. It's easier to move a short leg faster than a long one, but a long one covers more distance. Those are the trade-offs.

You don't have to be blessed to run at 90 strides per minute. Middle-sized people should reach 90 strides somewhere between a 7:00 and 6:30 pace. If you are tall, you might be at 85 strides; if you are shorter, you might be around 95. If your pace is slower than 7:00, then your concentration should go to simply moving your legs faster. Use a slightly shorter stride more often. You should have the sense that you are landing over your foot. Once you can run faster than 6:30 per mile at 90 strides per minute, your biggest increases will then come from stride distance or pushoff. You will need to concentrate on the end of your running stride and developing a more forceful pushoff. Hill repeats will help.

First, you need to establish your current stride rate at race pace. After a long warm-up, run for 10 minutes at what you feel is a 10K race effort without the cycling leg. Count either your right or left footstrikes for a minute early in the 10-minute period and then again later after about 8 minutes. It's best if you can also establish your pace so you have that as a reference. If you get slower at the end, but your count stays the same, then you have lost distance per stride. If your count goes down, then your turnover has slowed. To race faster, you then need to go out and fix this.

The cycling leg of the triathlon slows down your running. A good round figure is obtained by subtracting about 10 percent from the speed that you are able to run when fresh. Cycling involves a more forceful contraction than running. So most people will lose some force in their running pushoff after a bike leg. Your stride will be shorter by 5 to 10 percent. If your stride rate drops another 10 percent, you have probably slowed your pace about a minute and a half per mile—almost 10 minutes in a 10K. It shouldn't be that much. Running is still running, and even though your legs are tired, the rules haven't changed. The paces above still hold. If you are slower than a 6:30 to 7:00 pace, then your means to a faster run split is to move your legs more quickly. If you have been pushing a big gear at 80 rpm on the bike for the last hour or so, it's a tough trick to get your legs to move any faster. Try it sometime. Your legs won't want to go over 80 strides per minute. A faster cycling cadence may not get you down the road any faster, but it should be easier. Come off the bike after a cadence of 90, and your legs will be able both to turn over faster and push off harder. Anything that you do is habit forming. Practice a particular leg turnover, and they will keep doing it. If your legs can keep moving, you will finish sooner.

During a race, if you notice that your run pace begins to fade, it usually means that your turnover has slowed. We'll get into race fueling in the next chapter, but you might also be running low on carbohydrates. If you have to shorten your stride to maintain turnover, whether in training or in racing, do so. Try gradually to push off a little bit harder to get back up to pace.

It will happen in training, so you will have an opportunity to practice.

It doesn't take long to make changes in turnover. In cycling, all you need to do is choose a lower gear. It's not necessary to know your cadence at all times. It's probably better just to get a feel for it. Most people, when told to hold an L4 level on a flat stretch of road, will pedal between 90 and 95 rpm on their own. It's the easiest way to go fast, and we are all lazy. We do anything the easiest way possible. Count your cadence sometime and see.

Running turnover is a little more difficult, but if you work on the forward lean described in the last chapter, you'll find that it will also come naturally.

Drills for Turnover

The following drills will help increase your turnover.

Downhill running. Do 5 to 10 repeats for 30 seconds with 2 minutes of recovery. Don't pick an extremely steep hill; a moderate slope (less than 8%) is best. Practice leaning forward without bending at the waist. It's a foot-to-head, whole-body lean. Let gravity pull you and make your feet keep up. Caution: This can be hard on knees, ankles, and back, especially if you have had prior problems.

Fast run pickups. During an easy run, do four to five fast running pickups for 20 seconds, with complete recovery. Try to get to 95 strides.

200-meter running. Do 10 to 15 repeats of 200-meter fast runs (95-plus stride rate) with 200-meter recovery jogs.

Drills for Stride Distance

Use the following drills to help lengthen your stride distance.

Hip hyperextension. This is a resistance exercise. You can use stretch cords hooked to something solid about six inches high. Hook the other end around your ankle. Pull your leg back through a running motion. Do three sets of 15 repetitions. You should feel this in the hamstrings and glutes.

Uphill runs. Run uphill for 2 minutes six to eight times. Pick a slope on which you can maintain your turnover. Jog for 2 minutes between repeats.

Moderate running.   Do 10 to 12 minutes of moderate running, 5 minutes of easy running, and then 10 to 12 minutes at race effort running up a slight grade. Those with small children can push a baby jogger. Keep turnover at race count.

Combo.   Run for 40 to 50 minutes over rolling terrain. Do 2 minutes of hard effort in some up sections. Run fast for 2 minutes in some down sections. Alternate hard efforts with 2 minutes of easy running.

9

TIME-SAVING RACING

This chapter gets down to what this is all about—racing. Don't get me wrong. I think training is fun. Training with friends is a great social outing. And when you do all this just for the personal satisfaction of doing something better, you'll get more out of it. But racing is where the true exhilaration comes in. The training gets you fit, but the charge and the high come from racing. You don't have to compete with anyone but yourself. We are all our toughest competitors anyway. Winning is crossing old barriers.

Like all good things, there is a limit to effective racing. People seem to forget that racing is training time. It's also your hardest training. You will never go out and train at the same level you race. There just isn't the same motivation in training. I suppose if every workout were published and passed around to all your friends and the evening news, you might go a little harder. But the rest of the time, if you can increase your effort on a continuing basis, you are doing well.

HOW MUCH RACING?

Some people can race more often than others. Racing two weeks in a row at sprint or intermediate distances may produce a better second race than first race. Some people can do international distance races every week for several weeks. More typically, the third race in a row is a little flat, and the fourth goes straight to the toilet. Racing is the most specific training you can do. The days between races are short training days, so you are saving gobs of time and having fun on the weekend.

Most people seem to be able to tolerate one or two international distance or sprint races per month over a four- to six-month period. Some intersperse these with 10Ks, open-water swim races, and bike centuries. You reach a plateau after a couple of months of more than two events per month. You can get through a season of an event every weekend, but your improvement curve will flatten out. And you may get slower.

Longer races are another story. Recovery from half-Ironman races is usually complete in a couple of weeks. But it can take six weeks or longer to recover from an Ironman. A couple of half-Ironman races with a few international distance races is usually no problem. One Ironman a year is plenty. Most people who do Ironman distance races as habit won't do one every year. They may do one each year for a couple of years and then just do shorter races for a year or until they change age groups. There are people who do more, but ask them how they feel. Tired, all the time.

There is always the temptation to think that if you do longer races, you will be stronger for shorter distances. I haven't seen it yet. I've even tried it myself. It didn't work. It may not hurt your short-race performance, but it won't help. Shorter races will help both to raise your threshold and to minimize threshold drift, which will carry over to longer distances. Longer distance races tend to bring residual fatigue. So if you are going to do the long stuff, you will do well to race international and sprint distance races.

TWO-WEEK CRASH TRAINING

Perhaps you bought this book in the fall and have been following all this wonderful advice. Now it is spring and you are fully prepared to race. You can skip this and go to the tapering section. This section is for procrastinators. You may have a race coming up in a couple of weeks and you are having your first look at all this wisdom. Your training has been sporadic. Or you've read up to this point, but have ignored my advice, and now you say, "Train me in three weeks." Congratulations, you are normal. Here's your second chance to pull off a decent race. Of course it can't be as good as if you had been doing gradual improvement, sport rotations, and training your weaknesses. But you can still beat your friend who hasn't been training either. Researchers have some good news for procrastinators. In just a few weeks, you can boost your performance by as much as 4 percent. It's not easy, but it can be done.

Scientists show that you can enhance running performance through intense cycling training. That means that you can maintain swimming, increase your cycling and running effort, and race faster with little change in your overall training time. Because you will spend most of your race on the bike and run, the crash plan won't even attempt to make an improvement in

A group of riders leaves the transition area of the Vineman.

your swimming ability. If you haven't been doing any swimming, you should at least get yourself to the point that you can finish the distance without too much fatigue. Try a modification of week 1 in chapter 6.

Procrastination training works to improve both your running and cycling primarily through an intensified cycling schedule. This plan is a time saver; it works, but you will become tired. To make the change, you will need to double your effort. The additional stress may put you on the fine line of overtraining. If you carry it out too long, you will become overtrained and possibly injured. Don't train like this for very long. Not everyone can do it all. If you're still game, read on. A new adventure awaits.

There are a couple of ways to do it. You already know that fitness cycles tend to run in two- to three-week patterns. This plan attempts to make full use of that principle. The short plan builds for two weeks and then backs off the week before your event. The longer plan is to build for two or three weeks, go easy for a week, build again for two weeks, and then taper for a week. You could integrate the long plan into two races, three weeks to a month apart, at the end of the easy weeks. Most people will plateau at that point. If that happens, change your emphasis to swimming and give your legs a rest for a week or two.

The key to this plan is to double your cycling time at or near threshold. Some people can also do the same on the run, but be careful. Overtraining and injuries come more quickly with running. The plan will still work if you add half of your threshold time to your first run week. Then do a little more on the second week. The third week is easy. In the easy week, you can still do the interval workouts but cut them in half, or even down to a third.

First, you need to do some calculating. You should know your threshold to make the best use of this plan. If you've skipped to this chapter, go back to chapter 2 to calculate your threshold.

Procrastination training assumes that you are currently cycling less than four hours a week and running less than three hours a week. Most people who do one day a week of intervals will spend 5 to 10 percent of their time in that state of extreme happiness. Under the crash plan, you will need at least two days of intervals or threshold training on the bike.

Let's first put together a hypothetical week before a crash course. You have two to three workouts on the bike and two to three running. You like to get out for longer training on the weekends. In typical bike training, when you add up your pulls and climbing time, a two-hour group ride with hills often produces 10 minutes of threshold riding. An hour workout with intervals of equal work and rest time will produce another 10 to 20 minutes. If you have another moderate ride of an hour, the base week is four hours with 20 minutes of total threshold time, or 8 percent. To turn this into a crash week, double the number of repeats during the interval workout and replace the moderate ride with a 20-minute time trial. You have increased your threshold time to 40 to 50 minutes, or 17 to 21 percent. It is important to do the bike intervals at 90 rpm or above. You want to move your legs on the bike at least as fast as you do on the run. Standing on hills at as fast a cadence as you can handle will transfer to running strength. If you are accustomed to doing higher intensity workouts, you can put two or even three of these workouts on successive days. Usually this works better in the second week. Cycling, because it produces no landing impact, is a better way to increase your threshold time than running.

The base run week might include an hour fartlek or an interval session of 10 minutes at threshold, another moderate run of 45 minutes, and a longer run of 60 to 90 minutes. This would be a week with threshold time of 6 percent. To turn this into a crash program, have an interval session with 1- to 2-minute threshold efforts and turn the moderate run into three to five alternating 5-minute efforts. Do 5 minutes at just below threshold followed by 5 minutes of easy running. This all takes your threshold time up to 12 percent. Immediate changes will come not so much from an increase in training time but from an increase in time at threshold.

If you haven't been doing any kind of threshold training, but have at least been active, integrate 20 percent of your total cycling and 10 percent of your run time to threshold work. Don't increase your total training time the first week. But add 20 to 50 percent the second week and slightly increase your threshold time. You can tolerate this kind of increase probably no longer than two weeks before you need to back off. A week when you cut your workouts in half should allow recovery. If it is a race week, it is better to taper the effort.

You can take your percentage time at threshold up to as much as 40 percent as long as you were at 20 percent before your crash course. You simply double from your present point for two weeks. Some people can even go as high as 50 percent. You can probably change a performance level before you have truly adapted to the increased training stress. It takes time to adjust completely. Pay close attention to your overall energy level and health. A sore throat, a cold, or severe muscle soreness indicates an immune system suppression. You will need to ease off. The training simply won't work.

A couple of sample weeks are shown on the first two tables at the end of this chapter. You will see that they are similar to the cycling emphasis weeks shown in chapter 6. The difference between an emphasis week and a crash week is the increase in threshold time from recent training. An increase up to 50 percent is an emphasis. More than that constitutes crash training.

It's better to intensify your cycling time than to add running miles. It sounds crazy, but this plan can work when you actually cut back on running time. If you are reluctant to do that, go ahead and maintain your running but be sure to increase the intensity on the bike. This can still increase your running performance.

HEART RATE AND FUEL DURING RACING

If you go faster, your heart rate rises. If you go slower, it drops. That sounds simple enough, but there is more to it than that. During a race, you want to watch for the trends discussed in chapter 3. The longer the race, the more important this is. Things seldom go according to plan in any arena. Midrace adjustments in a triathlon can get you out of trouble and to the finish line more quickly with greater comfort.

The Heart: A Brief Job Description

During hard exercise, the heart pumps around 30 liters per minute. As you begin to exercise, adrenaline makes your heart beat faster to keep up with the demand of your exercising muscles. Then, as your core temperature rises, so will your heart rate. This is because the pumping capacity (stroke volume) of the heart diminishes with increases in internal temperature. Under normal conditions, your core temperature will reach 101 degrees Fahrenheit. The muscles themselves can go up to about 104 degrees. These are normal heat conditions, and you can expect an elevated heart rate.

All sorts of things are going on as blood surges around your system. Nutrients are picked up and delivered. Oxygen and carbon dioxide are exchanged, and lactic acid is shuttled around. The heart doesn't care what you are doing. All it knows is to keep up with blood demand. You need a full tank of blood to perform to your potential. If your tank starts to empty, you will have problems.

Fluids In and Out

Your fluid intake is a large factor in determining your blood volume. Blood is like any limited product. As conditions become more extreme, competition grows more intense. As you heat up, blood is diverted to the skin for cooling. But our muscles need all they can get. Your internal organs have given up their fair share, but your brain still diverts large quantities of blood to itself. The brain is selfish. The working muscles get less, but the heart does its best to compensate by beating faster. Under normal and healthy conditions, you can expect to see an increase of about 10 beats per minute at a given pace and level of exertion. In longer races, due to a partial dehydration there will also be a drop in blood volume, which will contribute to a heart rate rise.

With an increased sweat rate, your metabolism speeds up, which further contributes to a heart rate rise. Some people can sweat up to two liters per hour but can take in less than a liter. A certain amount of dehydration is acceptable. As long as you can replace 65 percent of your sweat loss, you will be all right. Aerobic metabolism produces a small amount of water, as much as 200 ml per hour. This can't keep you hydrated, but if you drink, the 200 ml can help. Experience has shown that drinking a liter or so an hour will keep you hydrated. This equates to two standard water bottles. It's best to drink continuously. You don't want to wait an hour and then chug a couple of water bottles. Absorption is better if you take in small amounts.

You have to sweat to stay cool. About 80 percent of the cooling that takes place is through the evaporation of sweat. Because your internal temperature is so high, any environmental temperature up to 104 degrees will still allow cooling. But you're getting into a very fine line, because if your internal temperature rises to 107 degrees, you can die. And it happens in triathlons.

When you begin to dehydrate, your blood volume drops. This will drastically increase your perceived effort, blood lactate levels, and glycogen depletion. Your heart works harder and harder to keep up, but with a reduced blood volume, it's pretty much a lost cause.

Putting on socks may take a few seconds, but it could save you minutes if your foot blisters later on.

There are early signs that you can monitor before trouble occurs. First we need to assume that you have hydrated yourself before your race to the point where your urine has been clear for at least a day. We also assume that you have cut back your training for at least a few days before the event so that your carbohydrate stores are up. If you start out dehydrated and glycogen depleted, you are in trouble.

Fuel In and Out

Much has been written and discussed about fat as a more desirable race fuel than carbohydrates. It's a tempting argument since we have around 90,000 calories of fat stored in our bodies. In endurance athletes, carbohydrates check in at

2,000 to perhaps 3,000 calories. Most of it is stored in the muscle cells as glycogen. People who regularly deplete their glycogen stores during training and then taper for a race while continuing to consume carbohydrates can super-compensate to over 3,000. Unfortunately, at a race effort (Ironman included) you will burn from 60 to 80 percent carbohydrates, 17 to 37 percent fat, and perhaps 3 percent protein. The faster you go, the higher the carbohydrate-to-fat ratio; in longer races the fat component rises. You may be able to increase your fat usage slightly, but it's not enough to make an appreciable difference in your race fueling or your regular diet.

A race effort will take between 500 and 1,000 calories per hour for most people. In theory, you can do an international distance race with no refueling. But you would be running close to an empty tank at the end. Experience has shown that it's better to top off the tank while you race. A sports drink or bar on the bike will help your effort later on the run.

Sports drinks of an 8 percent solution can supply both your carbohydrate and fluid needs if you take in close to a liter an hour.

In a half-Ironman or Ironman distance race, carbohydrate replenishment is an absolute necessity. You should start with a sports drink when you get on the bike and keep drinking until you get to the finish line. A standard water bottle full with an 8 percent solution of a sports drink will have 170 calories. If you drink two an hour, you will take in 340 calories. As long as you weren't depleted before you started, and you keep fueling, you should have enough carbs. You will use these ingested carbohydrates along with stored carbohydrates that give you about 200 to 300 more calories per hour. The faster you go, the more carbohydrates you will use, but you won't run out because you finish faster. The slower you go, the closer your intake and energy needs are to each other.

Using a Heart Rate Monitor to See the Trends

A heart rate monitor can help you keep a watch on your carbohydrate reserves and blood volume, especially in longer races because the trends become more evident. Let's say that you are going at a level that feels somewhat hard (L2), you have reached a steady pace, and your heart rate is 150 beats per minute. After an hour or so at this level, there will probably be a rise in heart rate due to heating. If it doesn't get over 160 and your pace and effort don't change, then everything is fine.

If your heart rate rises much over 10 beats from the baseline, to 165 for example, and the work is getting harder and you are slowing down, then you are probably beginning to dehydrate. You want to drink cool water. If you've been eating, don't drink a sports drink. That could further dehydrate you. The reason is that the food affects the osmolality in your gut so that water is being drawn from the bloodstream. You want to dilute the concentration so that water passes to the bloodstream. If you haven't taken anything in, and you've been out more than an hour, you are already behind. Try a sports drink and slow down. Then see if you get an energy lift after 15 minutes or so. After that, keep drinking. Take in as much as you can. It will be hard to drink more than you can absorb.

Let's look at the other side, which usually occurs at an hour and a half to two hours. Your heart rate begins to drop. It could happen during the run in an international distance race or in the later parts of the bike leg during a longer race. One of the results of fatigue is a desensitized heart response to adrenaline. You may have adrenaline running around your system, but your heart doesn't seem to notice or care. Your whole body is becoming tired. If you notice a big drop in pace and a rise in perceived effort, and your heart won't climb over 10 beats under the baseline, no matter how hard you try, then you are glycogen depleted. You have run out of fuel, bonked, hit the wall, and your body can no longer function as it should. You need carbohydrates and fast. A sports drink will fuel your system the most quickly. Cookies, candy bars, cola, sports bars—anything will work. Fruit doesn't work as well. If you have been drinking water, at least you won't be dehydrated on top of your other problems.

To make it all simple, watch for a heart rate rise of more than 10 beats, accompanied by a pace slowing and perceived effort rise. These symptoms indicate a need for fluids. Drink. If you experience a heart rate drop of more than 10 beats, you are running out of carbohydrate stores, and you need fuel. It's much easier to keep your tank topped off rather than let it go empty and then try to refill it. Everything works much faster, including your legs, if you keep your supply up.

TAPER

Everyone should taper. You don't have to be a high-performance athlete trying to peak for the Olympics. Tapering is a great way to rest. It will give you better races. Taper weeks take hardly any training time.

The longer your race, the longer your taper. A taper can involve a couple of things. One is simply reducing the amount of training that you do leading up to your event.

You should start tapering at least a month before an Ironman as long as you have had time to build your distances slowly. I like to have people do a five-hour bike followed by a three-hour run six weeks out from race day. Of course, they have to be ready for that much training in one day. If you haven't worked up to that range, then you can keep building until about three weeks before race day. You should start reducing your training about 30 percent the first week of your reduction. This gives you about 70 percent of your normal training. Then reduce about 20 percent a week up to the last week, which should be fairly limited no matter what your distance. For an Ironman race, you can taper for as long as six weeks. The last week should involve only two or three hours of training. Of course, your race then becomes part of your training week, so you should add that to your training total. But the training time itself is minimal.

If you have done one or more triathlons in the last year, the best way to identify your weak sport is to look at the race results and your relative placing in each segment.

For an international or sprint distance race, you can maintain regular training and then try the super taper the week leading into your event.

So now you've done everything just right to prepare for a race. The final touch is the last week. This is a tricky subject. The way people respond to a taper varies even more than training response. Some people perform better by training hard right up to their event. Those folks are rare. Most people respond better to a week of less training. Exactly how you do it may vary, but there is some convincing evidence that a higher intensity taper works best. You might want to reduce your time by 30 or 60 percent. Everyone should experiment a little with a taper. Any taper will be good for you. It won't hurt to taper even when you don't have a race, just to try it out and get your body used to the response. A taper week takes only about four hours of total training time, and you will usually wind up stronger at the end.

Of course a taper can work only if you reduce your training from a higher level. You can't be training three or four hours a week and then taper with a four-hour taper week like the one in this chapter. There must be a time reduction in both overall time and threshold time. Percentage of time at threshold may remain high, but the absolute time should be much less.

I have a plan that works well. It follows the approach of a study done a few years ago at McMaster University in Ontario.

The researchers looked at elite runners who reduced the number of 500-meter repeats throughout a week. They began with five on Monday, went to four on Tuesday, and continued reducing one per day until Friday. They rested Saturday and raced on Sunday. In all sorts of measures the runners improved. Similar high-intensity tapers used in other studies have also resulted in improved performance. One of the keys to performance that we touched on in the drinking section was blood volume. When it's down you don't perform well, but when it's up you perform better. So a taper must include enough intensity to maintain your blood volume. Only a couple of days of no training begins to cause a reduction in the blood tank. Higher intensity training stimulates a boost in blood volume, so a taper should have some L4 work. An excessive amount of training, however, will leave you glycogen depleted. By tapering the length of the workouts, your glycogen stores can become supercompensated. This is where people are different. The taper must balance both issues. If you have to make a mistake, it's better to train too little. It doesn't take very much to keep your blood volume up. You don't want to begin your race with a half tank of glycogen. You can take the taper in the last table at the end of this chapter and modify it to your needs.

Normal people should change a few things. You can take the McMaster findings and carry them over into all three sports. Because the training time is so short, you can do a variation of this taper in all three sports. Test athletes ran every day in the McMaster study, but it's not necessary as long as you are cycling. You can run two or three days and do the same with cycling and swimming. Rather than run a specific distance, you can just run one-minute L4 efforts with a rest of a minute and a half. That way you don't have to take the time to go to the track. Do them around the block. You can get on the stationary bike and do alternating minute-and-a-half efforts of L4 and L1 (very light). If you are doing a taper near the ocean or a lake, do the same with swimming for alternating minute or minute-and-a-half repeats. In the pool, do 50s or 100s with 15 to 30 seconds of rest.

Take Monday as a five-repeat day, Tuesday as a four, and so on to a one-repeat day on Friday if your race is on Sunday. If your race is on Saturday, make Thursday your one-repeat day. Most people seem to prefer to rest the day before an event, and logistically it's usually easier not to worry about it. If you like to train the day before an event, it's OK, but then make that your one-repeat day with rest the day before. Alternate your sports so that you follow a run day with a bike day and mix in three of the swim days when you can. A typical week is outlined in the last table at the end of this chapter.

PROJECTING RACE TIMES

You can use the tests outlined in chapter 2 to estimate where you are headed in a race. Part of it depends on your race distance. To make your projections, you need to be comfortable training near the length of time that you expect to be racing. If you have never ridden longer than two hours at a time, the projections are fine for a sprint or international distance race. But you are going to have some trouble in a half-Ironman or Ironman distance event. For an Ironman race, your preparation must have included at least two five-hour bike rides and two three-hour runs to project a race accurately. (There are many mysteries and adventures in long races.) You only need to do these longer training sessions once per week. Increase the distance gradually, about 10 percent per week. The best system is to make these increases every other week up to about a month before your event. If you are comfortable with a two-hour bike ride and one-hour run, your distance work for international or sprint distance races is covered. In swimming, you should be able to complete a set of five 200-meter repeats with 30 to 60 seconds of rest to feel comfortable with a sprint or international distance race. You should be able to do 10 of them for an Ironman. Three swim sessions a week totaling three hours will enable you to finish with dignity.

In figuring how long you should spend in a race, you need to remember the snowballing effect from weak swimming or cycling. If your swim leaves you fatigued, you cannot ride to your potential. If the bike leaves you tired, you can count on a slow run, no matter what kind of runner you are.

Performance Progress Plus will make race projections for you. If your times vary on your splits, you should look not only at the fitness of the slow segment but also at the one that preceded it. Performance Progress Plus can assess your fitness levels in all three sports to give you a little better insight about a training emphasis.

Swimming

Your 200s provide the best indicator of your fitness. The first thing to look for is whether you are able to maintain your time. If you can hold the same time on the last one as the first, then that will be close to your race pace for a half mile or mile. Two miles or more will make you slow from that pace three to five seconds per hundred meters. Your race pace should be fairly close to the time that you can maintain on the second-to-last 200.

If you can maintain 3 minutes 30 seconds on a set of 200-yard repeats, then you should be able to swim 1.5K in close to 28 minutes. Just take your time for a 200 and multiply it by eight.

The swim shouldn't leave you fatigued, so you should stay fairly comfortable. Three hours per week should be enough. You can get a little bit faster on the swim, but it usually takes doubling your training time, so the cost/benefit ratio is questionable.

Cycling

The first consideration is swimming. If you are fresh when exiting the water (or at least somewhat fresh), then a 5-minute cycling test will be a good indicator. Your pace at threshold for

5 minutes on a flat road with no wind will transfer to about a mile per hour slower over 40K, 2 to 3 miles per hour slower for 56 miles, and a little more than 4 miles per hour slower for 112 miles. If your pace fades as you get into the bike leg, then your distance work has been short, or you haven't done workouts—longer intervals and short time trials—to minimize your threshold drift.

Let's say that you can hold 21 miles per hour for 5 minutes and felt that you could have held the pace for another 10 minutes. That would be a good test. On a fairly flat course, with moderate or no wind, you should be able to average from 19 to 20 miles per hour for a 40K, depending on the course. Your time would be around 1:16. Your time for a 56-mile course would be close to 3:15. Your Ironman time would be 6:45.

Running

The run is where it gets tricky. This is the really interesting part of doing triathlons. You should be able to complete a swim and a bike leg as if the other didn't exist. Some people even ride better after a swim. When you get to the run, however, you know that you have been out there awhile, no matter what the distance of the event. Few people can run close to the pace that they run without a swim and bike beforehand.

In chapter 4 I mentioned the 10 percent rule of pace decline or time increase. If you can run a 42:00 10K, then your 10K in a triathlon should be no slower than 46:30. If you go beyond the 10 percent barrier, then your problem is more likely to be cycling than running. The bike leg took too much out of you. For a half-Ironman, you can figure on 15 percent. A 112-mile bike ride can slow your marathon pace by 20 percent.

To project your run, you first need to project your ability for a fresh run and then add percentage to the time. Mile repeats like those mentioned in chapter 2 provide a good indicator. The mile pace that you can repeat at least three times at a level of 14 on the Effort and Lactate Scale should be a pace that you take to your local 10K. So if your mile repeats are at a 7:00 pace, your projected 10K is 43:24. Your triathlon prediction using the 10 percent rule is 47:45. You can add about

30 seconds per mile for a half-marathon and 60 seconds per mile for a marathon. Then add the 15 or 20 percent for triathlon predictions. Performance Progress Plus makes all these projections for you. Of course these projections assume that you have run in training close to the length of time that you will in the race.

Once you race, you can look at your splits and determine if you need to emphasize one area to give it a short boost. During the season, you can go for a three-week cycle in one sport and plan on not losing anything in the other two. Running seems to be the least affected by a short maintenance cycle, as long as you continue training on the bike. Cycling improvements tend to come more quickly than improvements in the other two sports. Swimming fitness is the one most rapidly lost. The time-saving strategy is to maintain your strength so you are fresh to train your weakness.

	Swim	Bike	Run
MON	• 300 warm-up • 12 × 50 (mix strokes on odd #s, free on even #s) (20 s) • 6 × 100 build speed on even # laps (20 s) • 150 cool-down **45** min total **20** min L4	• Stationary • 5 min warm-up • 10 × 1 min L4 239 watts (1 min L1) • 5 min cool-down **30** min total **10** min L4	
TUES			• 10 min warm-up • 10 × 200 ~ 50 s (200 L1) keep running throughout workout • 10 min cool-down **40** min total **7** min L4
WED			
THURS	• 300 warm-up • 5 × 300 L2 (30 s) • 4 × 100 kick L2 (20 s) • 100 cool-down **55** min total **0** min L4	• 15 min warm-up • 10 mile hilly time trial • 15 min cool-down **60** min total **30** min L4	
FRI			• 10 min warm-up • 5 × 5 min L2.5 (45 s-1 min) Hr 164 • 10 min cool-down **45** min total **25** min L4
SAT			
SUN		• 2 hr L1 w/hills **120** min total **20** min L4	
	Total 1:40 **L4** 0:20 19.9%	**Total** 3:30 **L4** 1:00 28.5%	**Total** 1:25 **L4** 0:32 37.5%
		Weekly total 6:35	

Week 1 — Crash Week

	Swim	Bike	Run
MON	• 300 warm-up • 5 × 200 L4+ (1 min) • 5 × 100 L4+ (45 s) 1:48/100 • 5 × 50 L4+ (30 s) • 150 cool-down 50 min total 30 min L4		
TUES		• Stationary • 5 min warm-up • 7-10 × 2 min L2.5-L4 230 watts (1 min L1) • 5 min cool-down 40 min total 20 min L4	
WED		• 1 hr-1 hr 30 min L1 over rolling course, 15 × 30 s sprint uphill sections (full recovery) 90 min total 7 min L4	
THURS		• 1 hr L1 60 min total 0 min L4	• 10 min warm-up • 3-5 × 3 min L4 (3 min L1) • 10 min cool-down 50 min total 15 min L4
FRI			
SAT	• 300 warm-up • 3 × 500 at 1,500 m race pace 9:39/500 (1 min) • 4 × 150 kick/swim L2 (20 s) • 150 cool-down 60 min total 24 min L4		• 10 min warm-up & cool-down • 10 min L4 • 5 min L1 • 10 min L4 6:49 pace Hr under 173 39 min total 14 min L4
SUN		• 20 min L1 • 20 min L2 • 5 min L1 • 40 min L2.5-L4 21 mph Hr 159 • 30 min L1 115 min total 40 min L4	
	Total 1:50 **L4** 0:54 49.1%	**Total** 5:05 **L4** 1:07 22%	**Total** 1:29 **L4** 0:29 32.6%
		Weekly total 8:24	

Week 2 — Crash Week

	Swim	Bike	Run
MON	• 200 warm-up • 5 × 100 L4 (20 s) • 100 cool-down 20 min total — 7 min L4	• 10 min warm-up • 5 × 1:30 L4 (1:30 L1) • 5 min cool-down 30 min total — 7 min L4	
TUES	• 200 warm-up • 4 × 100 L4 (20 s) • 100 cool-down 22 min total — 6 min L4		• 10 min warm-up • 4 × 1 min L4 (1:30 L1) keep running • 5 min cool-down 25 min total — 4 min L4
WED		• 10 min warm-up • 3 × 1:30 L4 (1:30 L1) • 5 min cool-down 24 min total — 5 min L4	
THURS	• 200 warm-up • 2 × 100 L4 (20 s) • 100 cool-down 18 min total — 3 min L4		• 10 min warm-up • 2 × 1 min L4 (1:30 L1) keep running • 5 min cool-down 19 min total — 2 min L4
FRI	• 200 warm-up • 1 × 100 L4 (20 s) • 100 cool-down 16 min total — 2 min L4	• 10 min warm-up • 2 × 1:30 L4 (1:30 L1) • 5 min cool-down 19 min total — 1 min L4	
SAT			
SUN	• Race 1,500 meters 28:55 28 min total — 28 min L4	• Race 40K 1:09:57 69 min total — 30 min L4	• Race 10K 46:43 42 min total — 30 min L4
	Total 1:44 **L4** 0:46 44.2%	**Total** 2:22 **L4** 0:43 32.4%	**Total** 1:26 **L4** 0:36 41.9%
		Weekly total 5:32	

Index

A

Adrenaline, 161, 165
Aero bars, 134
Aerobic capacity. *See* $\dot{V}O_2$max (maximal aerobic capacity)
Aerobic energy, 4-6, 162
Aerodynamics, of cyclists, 86, 133-134
Age, and heart rate, 37-38
Aging process, 26
Alignment, in swimming, 119, 128
Amino acids, 50
Anaerobic energy, 4-6
Anaerobic threshold (AT), 6
Ankle inflexibility, of swimmers, 123-125
Arm rigidity, of cyclists, 133
Arm swing, of runners, 137

B

Back extension (exercise), 69
Base training, definition of, 11
"Belly breathing," 138
Bilateral breathing, by swimmers, 121
Blood lactate. *See* Lactic acid thresholds
Blood sugar, 48
Body fat, 163-164
Breathing
    bilateral, 121
    early, 121-122
    by runners, 138
    by swimmers, 121-122, 127
Butterfly stroke (swimming), 58

C

Carbohydrates, 5, 41, 48-49, 152, 163-164, 165-166
Carbon dioxide, 127, 138
Cardiovascular system
    response to cross training, 64-65
    strengthening of, 12
Co-contraction, 116
Combo (running drill), 154
Cool-downs, 25
Cortisol, 43, 44, 46
Crash training, 157-161, 173-174
Cross training, 64-65

Cycling
    favored in triathlons, 84
    in improvement phases, 61-63
    power in, 17-18, 62, 143-147
    proper form in, 129-134
    race times for, 170-171
    sample workouts for, 100-105
    seasonal rotation of, 56-57
    weekly schedule for, 78-79
    weight training exercises for, 67-69
Cycling cadence, proper, 133, 143, 150
Cycling test, as baseline, 30

D

Daniels, Jack, 149, 150
Dehydration, 41, 42, 162-163, 165
Diaphragm, breathing from, 138
Diet, balance in, 50
Dips (exercise), 72
Distance training
    addition of, 14-15
    drawbacks of, 9-12, 13, 47
Downhill running (drill), 153

E

Early breathing, by swimmers, 121-122
Effort and Lactate Scale, 6, 13, 20-23, 76, 85
Elbow locking, by cyclists, 133
Elite athletes
    appropriate training for, 10
    and illness, 45
    measuring improvements in, 31
Endurance
    and energy use, 4, 5
    and muscle strength, 66-67
Energy, 4-6, 13-14. *See also* Aerobic energy; Anaerobic energy

F

Fast run pickups (drill), 153
Fast-twitch muscle fibers, 4-5, 21, 26, 141, 147-148
Fat burning, in distance training, 9
Fatigue. *See also* Overreaching
    resistance to, 2, 18
    during triathlons, 141

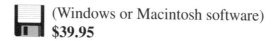

About the Author

Rick Niles is a highly experienced triathlon coach and an age-group triathlete. He has worked with athletes of all abilities since 1989. Niles holds regular triathlon training clinics in Santa Rosa, California, for age-group triathletes, and he coaches masters swimmers.

Overtrained, discouraged, and lacking a social life because of 20- and 30-hour training weeks during 1982 and 1983, Niles began to look for a better way. While earning an MA in physical education (with an exercise physiology concentration) from Sonoma State University (SSU), he developed his training system. He also taught assessment and conditioning classes for the general student population at SSU and for track and cross-country athletes.

Niles consults and designs training schedules for athletes all over the world. In addition to writing a software program called *Performance Progress Plus*, which assesses fitness levels and creates race projections for swimming, cycling, and running, Niles has written articles on training for *Runner's World*, *Bicycling*, and numerous regional publications. He is a regular contributor to *Inside Triathlon*, *Triathlete*, and *Triathlon Sports in Australia*.

Niles lives in Santa Rosa, California. In his free time he enjoys sailing, skiing, and spending time with his wife, Diane, and son, Kevin.